# THE TRUTH ABOUT

# CONFIDENT PRESENTING

James O'Rourke

PEARSON
Prentice Hall

Harlow, England • London • New York • Boston • San Francisco • Toronto
Sydney • Tokyo • Singapore • Hong Kong • Seoul • Taipei • New Delhi
Cape Town • Madrid • Mexico City • Amsterdam • Munich • Paris • Milan

PEARSON EDUCATION LIMITED

Edinburgh Gate
Harlow CM20 2JE
Tel: +44 (0)1279 623623
Fax: +44 (0)1279 431059
Website: www.pearsoned.co.uk

First published in Great Britain 2008

© Pearson Education Limited 2008

The right of James O'Rourke to be identified as author of this work has been asserted by him in accordance with the Copyright, Designs and Patents Act 1988.

ISBN: 978-0-273-71807-9

**British Library Cataloguing-in-Publication Data**
A catalogue record for this book is available from the British Library

Original edition, entitled TRUTH ABOUT CONFIDENT PRESENTING, THE, by O'ROURKE, JAMES, published by Pearson Education, Inc, publishing as FT PRESS, Copyright © 2008.

This edition published by PEARSON EDUCATION LTD, Copyright © 2008.

This edition is manufactured in Great Britain and is authorized for sale only in UK, EUROPE, MIDDLE EAST AND AFRICA.

10 9 8 7 6 5 4 3 2 1
12 11 10 09 08

Typeset in 10pt Meta Light LF by 3
Printed and bound in Great Britain by Ashford Colour Press Ltd, Gosport

The publisher's policy is to use paper manufactured from sustainable forests.

Harvard Business School professor John Kotter studied a number of successful general managers over a five-year period and found that they spend most of their time with other people, including subordinates, their bosses, and numerous people from outside the organization. His study found that the average manager spends just 25 percent of his time working alone. Most of that time with others, Kotter found, was spent talking and listening—and a sizable fraction was spent presenting ideas and actions to others.

Similarly, management consultant Dierdre Borden found that successful managers spend about 75 percent of their time in verbal interaction with others: on the telephone, face-to-face, in meetings, and in presentations to large and small groups. The fact is, most information in contemporary business and social settings is passed orally, and our most important ideas are frequently formalized in presentations to clients, customers, shareholders, superiors, and key decision makers.

You can't avoid it. At some point soon in your career, you're going to be asked to give a presentation. The problem is that most people are genuinely apprehensive about doing that. We can compose a memo, letter, report, or e-mail in the quiet and comfort of our home or office, but standing in front of a group to offer our thoughts—or to motivate them to action—is simply frightening to many people.

Like it or not, during a presentation you're being evaluated by everyone in the audience. You're being sized up, critiqued, and assessed. For those 15 or 20 minutes, your value to the organization, your career...your future are on the line. No wonder people get nervous.

I've been teaching public speaking to business school students, government and military officials, and professionals in all lines of work for more than 35 years, and I've learned one simple truth about public speaking: It's not easy, but it's certainly doable. I've helped people overcome fears, anxieties, and apprehensions of all sorts and watched them go on to wow an audience with their presentation skills. If they can do it, so can you.

This book, simple and compact as it is, can do three things for you. First, it can help you to diagnose your current speaking abilities.

It can help you size up your skill levels and get some sense of whether you're "ready for prime time." Second, it shows you the standards of the North American marketplace. Point-by-point, you find the expectations of the business and professional world. Finally, this book gives you the toolkit you need to prepare, improve, and present. It's all here, neatly tucked into 51 Truths.

The most important truth to be learned, however, is this: Great presenters weren't born that way. They became great by focusing on their message, the needs of the audience, the pattern of organization, and the details of presenting. Persistence, dedication, and a little practice can go a long way toward making you a top-notch public speaker. The details are straight ahead.

TRUTH

# 1

## Public speaking is not easy, but it's certainly doable

If you've ever had to make a presentation, you know the anxiety that comes with speaking in public. Even experienced speakers can feel flustered, sweaty, anxious, and apprehensive. That's a perfectly natural reaction to a seemingly threatening situation. And when you know you're being evaluated, you feel even more threatened. Your perception of a threat causes you to release adrenal fluids, dilate your pupils, tense your muscles, and provokes a "fight or flight" response. You understand the consequences of not doing well, of failing to impress an audience, or not coming through for a client when it really matters. You know all too well what can go wrong.

Good public speakers tend to focus on what can go right. They concentrate on the positive aspects of their message and how it can benefit their audience. Once they detect a positive response from their listeners, that perception serves to reinforce a sense of self-confidence, reassurance, and belief that they can do this.

The fact is, public speaking is a *learned* skill. It's not something you're born with or that comes naturally. You're certainly born with the propensity to speak and gesture, but given the short range of the human voice, those skills are clearly intended for interpersonal or small-group settings. Speaking to a larger audience is a skill that must be learned, rehearsed, and reinforced through repeated opportunities.

> Good public speakers tend to focus on what can go right. They concentrate on the positive aspects of their message and how it can benefit their audience.

Keep this in mind: Very few small children are great public speakers. So how do young managers (and others) get to be so good at presenting complex information to an audience that has little interest or motivation in learning? More to the point, how do they get the audience to act on the message being shared? The answer, in part, lies in the response to the classic New York pedestrian's question, "How do I get to Carnegie Hall?" The response? "Practice, practice, practice."

People with very little natural ability have become exceptional public speakers by the time they reach their twenties and thirties. Great orators, politicians, and business leaders develop professional speaking skills by analyzing both their audience and their purpose for speaking. They prepare meticulously and seek out opportunities to present; then they learn what is effective from the audiences' feedback.

Every speaker who is honest with you will admit to being anxious or nervous before a presentation. Entertainers and comedians like the late Johnny Carson and David Letterman have talked at length about the anxiety that accompanies a walk onto the stage to perform. There is a subtle difference between them and most speakers-in-training. Experienced presenters use that sense of apprehension to their advantage: They review their notes, they think about what the audience expects of them, they rehearse their opening lines, and they internalize the essence of their message. They are, in a word, prepared.

Great speakers may seem to perform with an ease that makes it all look effortless, but the most honest of them will tell you that it didn't come easily. It requires dedication, discipline, and a commitment to improve. You can do the same. The moment to begin is now.

TRUTH

2

The key to success is preparation

Effective preparation for a presentation involves more than practice, but it's all relatively easy if you take it step-by-step.

In the fourth century B.C., the Greek philosopher Aristotle gathered his students around him near the city of Athens and passed along a small bit of wisdom: Things will go better during a speech if you're properly prepared. In a collection of his lectures, passed by oral tradition for many years and later written down as his *Rhetoric*, Aristotle explains that three considerations are particularly important for every speaker: audience, purpose, and occasion.

*Audience* clearly comes first. A presentation is all about them. It doesn't matter what you want. It doesn't matter how interesting, important, or powerful *you* think

# All that really matters is what the audience wants.

your message is. All that really matters is what the audience wants. If you can't deliver a presentation that they find interesting, engaging, useful, valuable, or worth thinking about, then your audience will ignore you. They may be polite, of course. They may nod, smile, and appear interested, but deep inside they're thinking about something else. They're tuned in to their own needs and interests, not yours. You must figure out what they want or need and give it to them. Your reward is their undivided attention and, perhaps, the behavior you're hoping for.

Your *purpose* matters, as well. Consider these questions: Why are you speaking to *this* group, on *this* occasion, about *this* topic? What's your reason for being here? You may think it's to sell a product, a concept, or an idea. You may have something in mind for the audience to do (or stop doing). But your purpose is subtler than that. You should know what your intended outcome is. Aristotle gives three reasons why a speaker might address an audience: to inform, to persuade, or to inspire. Some presentations call for all three; others focus on just one. What you choose to do depends on the outcome you envision for this particular audience.

Distinguish between informative and persuasive purposes as you prepare. If your purpose is to inform, you can't become an advocate on behalf of only one point of view, and you can't gratuitously toss in your opinions along the way. On the other hand, if you hope to influence what the audience believes or does, then figure out not only how to motivate them to care about the subject, but also how to offer evidence that they find compelling.

# Distinguish between informative and persuasive purposes as you prepare.

Some years ago, I was an officer in the United States Air Force and assigned to a strategic refueling base in eastern Canada. Each week, as the wing staff gathered in the conference room to brief the commander on issues and actions in the organization, we received a detailed weather briefing from the wing meteorologist. He always came prepared with charts, graphs, and maps, complete with occluded fronts, low-pressure systems, and more. He even carried an authoritative-looking collapsible pointer. He told us in exquisite detail what happened yesterday, what was likely to happen in the next 24 to 48 hours, and what the five-day prediction would be. No matter how bad the weather was forecast to be (and Labrador was noted for some ferocious storms), he would never direct the commander to relocate the tanker fleet. That wasn't his job. His task was purely informative. He supplied the information that the commander and the senior staff required and let them engage in persuasive conversation. Recognizing his proper role in that situation (and making accurate forecasts) kept our young weather officer out of trouble and in the commander's good graces.

Finally, the *occasion* matters, too. In addition to knowing who will hear your talk and the purpose for your presentation, it may also be useful for you to know something about the occasion. Many situations simply call for a polite, informative presentation. Others require that you incorporate some theme into your speech that arises from the moment. Certain holidays can lend a clear and useful tone to your talk, such as Christmas ("Peace on Earth, goodwill toward all."), Thanksgiving ("We are grateful for what we have been given and mindful of those who have less."), or Independence Day ("The price of freedom is eternal vigilance.").Preparing yourself by thinking about your audience, purpose, and the occasion won't guarantee success, but it will certainly increase your odds.

# TRUTH

3

## Rehearsal is essential

We're all asked to speak on occasion without benefit of any rehearsal (give an impromptu talk), but on those occasions, the audience knows that you've just been asked to "say a few words." Their expectations are low and the demands of the occasion won't ask much of you.

If your presentation involves anything more than a brief introduction of someone else, you had better prepare yourself by rehearsing the talk—more than once. If you care about the outcome, don't even consider showing up for the speech without rehearsing your remarks.

Rehearsal provides at least three benefits for your speech. First, it points out potential timing problems. You will know after a run-through or two of your talk whether you have too much, too little, or just enough to say. Is timing important? It's crucial, actually. In most North American business meetings, the senior person in the room speaks last. That means, of course, that junior members of the organization speak first. If their presentations run long or if they overstay their welcome, then the most important folks in the room will have less time to speak than they had planned, which is never a pleasant situation.

> If you care about the outcome, don't even consider showing up for the speech without rehearsing your remarks.

A few years ago, I was asked to join the corporate communication team of The Boeing Company for a meeting in the company's Chicago headquarters. The meeting began well with a few brief presentations by junior project managers and section chiefs. One young woman in the employee communication division, however, was given eight minutes to brief the group on her recent activities and instead took twenty. By the time the meeting came around to Judith Muhlberg, the senior vice president for corporate communication, very little time was left and the CEO had yet to make his remarks. "I didn't get to be a senior executive in this company by taking other people's speaking time," she said, "so let me make this very brief." After just a couple of minutes, she turned the floor over to her chief executive, making sure he had his full allocation of time to speak. Following the meeting, Ms. Muhlberg collared the young project manager in the hallway and let her know in no uncertain terms what she thought about her presentation. As a three meter (ten foot) space cleared out around the two of them, it was obvious the young lady from employee communication was having what some managers call "a career moment" with her boss.

The second benefit that a rehearsal provides is improvement in your transitions. As you practice your speech, you can identify the rough spots and work on transitioning clearly from one main point to another. You may be confronted with words, ideas, or terminology you don't understand. (You have a choice here: Figure it out or don't use it). A word or phrase may look good when you write your speech on a laptop, but then you realize that it just doesn't sound right for one reason or another. Some words appeal more to the eye than the ear, and it's during rehearsal that you'll discover these problems.

Finally, a rehearsal helps you polish your delivery and build confidence. As you become familiar with the words, phrases, and concepts in your talk, you'll internalize their meaning and become more self-assured about speaking aloud in front of an audience. Rehearsal improves your pacing and phrasing, as well.

*Pacing* is the rate at which you speak—how many words per minute you utter. Keep in mind that most conversations take place at around 125 to 140 words per minute. In a large auditorium with voice amplification, you may want to slow down. You may also want to slow down if the subject of your speech is technical, complex, or unfamiliar to the audience. *Phrasing* means you choose where to pause, stop, breathe, and begin again. Once you're thoroughly familiar with the content of your speech, you'll feel better about knowing where to pause, when to breathe, and how long to be silent before you begin the next thought.

When you rehearse, stand up and speak out loud. Don't hold back. Do all that you can to create the impression in your mind that the audience is right there waiting to hear from you. Time yourself as you practice and mark on your manuscript (if you're using one) which words to emphasize and where to pause. If you plan to use notes, make them simple, compact, easy-to-follow, numbered, and readable. Keep in mind that your audience doesn't want you to read to them, they want you to speak to them. We'll explore more about

# Every rehearsal is one more opportunity to build skill and confidence.

working with notes and manuscripts later. Just keep in mind that every rehearsal is one more opportunity to build skill and confidence. Believe me, it pays big dividends when the occasion arrives.

TRUTH

4

Emulating good speakers
makes you better

A learning curve charts the learning progression of someone who is acquiring a new skill. Educational psychologists find that most learners experience a slow rate of progress at first, followed by a rapid acceleration of new knowledge or ability, followed in turn by a flattening of the curve as time progresses. In other words, most students typically struggle at first with the concepts, vocabulary, and processes involved in learning a new skill. Many discouraged students think about quitting. Consider, for example, when you tried to learn how to play the piano or ride a bicycle. Acquiring a complex motor skill requires discipline, patience, and dedication.

Research on public speaking shows two basic phenomena related to learning. First, a concentrated program of instruction, rehearsal, and critique can produce significant improvements in performance in a relatively short period of time. And second, the confidence acquired early in the process can result in higher levels of achievement over time.

The lessons from these findings are simple. Learning to present in public is much easier, for example, than learning to write or becoming an informed, critical listener. Confidence also plays a huge role in motivating inexperienced speakers to continue speaking, practicing, and to accept the challenge of presenting under stressful, high-stakes conditions. You gain confidence with every successful presentation, which inspires you to take on other opportunities and take additional risks. The process begins with instruction, which really means watching and listening to successful speakers. People who can stand up and present successfully in front of others—offering compelling stories, dramatic narrative, or powerful evidence—seem at first to be relatively rare. Most of us don't know many people who are that good, but I'm willing to bet that you know more of these people than you think.

Think about the best speakers you know, the ones who are *always* good when they get up to speak. My local church has an assistant rector who is really good. When he gives a homily on Sunday, he doesn't step up in the pulpit and read from a set of prepared remarks. He steps down in front of the altar, with nothing to hide behind and nothing to take his eyes off the congregation, and speaks to us. He's confident, full-throated, and full of enthusiasm. The experience is almost always high-energy, both for him and for the audience. Often, he begins with a story about a recent event or about some people he's just met. Sometimes, he gives a narrative about events from his childhood, which he then links to the biblical readings for the day.

What makes him such a good speaker? For one thing, he isn't reading to us. He isn't preaching, either. He's having a conversation with the people in his church, sharing some small bit of wisdom he thinks will improve their lives. Furthermore, he's rehearsed his homily to the point where he isn't likely to forget what he's going to say; he knows what transitions work and where to pause for breath. He also understands how to keep it moving, when to pause and gather our attention, and when to deliver the next point. Honestly, he's fun to listen to, even if you've heard this particular story before. He's informative, he's persuasive, and he's inspiring all at the same time. And—here's a real benefit he probably hadn't intended—he's instructive.

Those of us who think about presenting and public speaking are taking mental notes while he speaks. The more astute among the congregation are saying to themselves, "That's how to organize an anecdote in support of a main point," or "That's how to keep an audience involved in the message." Some folks are thinking about other things: unpaid bills, the new car they'd like to buy, or events in the week ahead. Still others are engaged in food fantasies or fighting the urge to sleep. But more people are paying attention to this particular speaker than most, simply because he's skilled at the task of presenting.

> Look at a listening opportunity as a learning opportunity and take careful mental notes.

Rather than tell yourself, "I'll never be as good as he is," ask yourself, "What can I learn from someone this gifted?" Look at a listening opportunity as a learning opportunity and take careful mental notes. Not all lessons are positive. Occasionally, you come across a bad speaker (someone forced to stand up and report on a task she would clearly have rather written an e-mail about), and you say to yourself, "Egad! I'm glad I don't do *that* when I speak." Or "That's one thing I'll never do when it's my turn to present." Those lessons are just as important as the positive, high-energy teaching points from well-practiced speakers. In 2007, Microsoft Chairman Bill Gates delivered the commencement address at Harvard University. In preparation, Gates read the 1947 address given by then-Secretary of State George C. Marshall, in which he outlined the *Marshall Plan*, the bold economic-relief program that lifted Europe from the ashes of World War II. In his own speech, Gates incorporated a number of Marshall's words and ideas, helping to shape his own vision of the world that new college graduates will face. Gates made the speech his own, but he certainly recognized a successful approach and a gifted speaker in General Marshall. One more suggestion: As you listen to the best speakers you can identify in your community, formulate some questions that focus on what you'd most like to learn from them and approach them with brief, polite inquiries about how they do it. I think you'll find many of them approachable, instructive, and more than willing to offer advice.

# TRUTH

# 5

# Establish goals for your presentation

If you're going to ask people to sit through a presentation (or if they are forced to do so by your employer), then you ought to give them one or more good reasons for doing so. Those reasons are almost always directly related to the second of Aristotle's considerations: purpose. Ask yourself, "Why are you speaking, and what can the audience hope to gain from listening to you?"

Let's begin with a review of your goals for the presentation. You don't have any goals? Well, you should back up and think about that first. What do you want to achieve from this presentation? Remember, the answer to this question must be related to the needs and interests of your audience. Presumably, you want to help them learn, understand, or appreciate something. You may be trying to help them do something in particular. The success of your presentation is best measured against how well the audience understands or appreciates the subject once you finish speaking. Or, perhaps, how well they can do what you've instructed them to do. Remember, if you don't meet your big-picture goals—your reasons for speaking to a particular group—then the clever organization and good delivery of your talk don't matter at all.

In defining your goals or objectives for a speech, the first rule is to "Limit yourself to one sentence." If you need more than one sentence to state your goal, then you're not clear about your objective. Here's an example: "The objective of this speech is to convince my audience that increased free cash flow will result in a healthier balance sheet." This objective is nicely focused and reasonably direct. You might have to define a few terms and then explain how it all works, but it does fit into one sentence. The problem, of course, is that it's not very specific. Here's another example of a goal: "I hope to convince my audience that reducing the age of accounts receivable to 30 days or less makes the company more profitable." This objective is more specific and lends itself to measurement. Once you explain the terms and show the audience how accounts receivable aging works, then you can show the relationship to profitability.

> If you need more than one sentence to state your goal, then you're not clear about your objective.

The second rule of goal setting is, "Make sure the objective is realistic." Asking for too much, too soon may set you up for failure. Make sure your objective is well within the comfort zone of your audience. If you're asking for something that exceeds their comfort level, it won't matter how glib you are because they'll simply reject your argument. The third rule is, "Make sure that both you and your audience are clear on what you want to achieve." You should distinguish between informative and persuasive objectives, and make certain your audience knows what you want them to understand or do. The result will be a presentation that will be relatively easy to judge. You'll have fair and simple measures of success.

Clearly defined objectives provide other benefits, as well. First, setting goals helps you to determine whether you actually need to give a presentation. There may well be a simpler, easier, less expensive way to transfer information to your audience. Second, clearly defined objectives can help you to focus the attention and energy of your audience. You should know both why you're speaking to them and what you each can expect as a result. Third, clearly defined objectives allow you to focus on the audience's needs rather than your own. Remember, this is all about them. This idea may seem counterintuitive, but it's true. Finally, a clearly defined objective is the only way to measure the success of your presentation. And without an objective, one result is just as good as another.

> Make sure your objective is well within the comfort zone of your audience.

# TRUTH

6

# A presentation is a learning occasion

Each presentation is a learning opportunity for your audience. They may be revisiting familiar concepts and ideas, or they may be exploring uncharted territory. But for everyone seated in front of you, your presentation is an opportunity to learn something new or reinforce previous learning.

In the middle of the last century, a college professor by the name of Benjamin Bloom led a group of his colleagues in examining how people learn. One of their most useful observations was a classification system used to examine various types of learning. In their study of university students across the United States, they found that learning falls broadly into three categories:

- **Knowledge**—Mental skills that involve the direct transfer of information about a subject from speaker to listener.

- **Attitude**—Growth in feelings or emotional areas. This results in greater appreciation or valuing of the subject.

- **Skills**—Manual or physical skills. The skills may be as complex as learning to sail or as simple as learning to ride a bicycle.

You need to think about the objectives of your presentation in terms of what you want your audience to learn. Learning to appreciate abstract expressionism or fine wines is a much different experience from learning how to swim or how to do your annual tax return. Let's focus on the first two of these learning categories and begin with the knowledge domain. Bloom and his colleagues defined a hierarchy of understanding that moves from basic, elementary stages of learning to highly advanced levels. As you establish your objectives for a presentation, think about which of the following levels of learning might be most appropriate for your audience:

- **Knowledge**—This level includes the most basic forms of observation and recall of information. This might include knowledge of dates, events, places, and major ideas.

- **Comprehension**—This level involves more than basic recall; it entails an understanding of what the facts mean, along with an ability to translate knowledge into a new context. Your audience should be able to interpret facts, compare, contrast, infer causes, and predict consequences.

■ **Application**—At this level, an audience can use information, methods, concepts, and theories in new situations. They can solve problems using required skills and knowledge.

■ **Analysis**—This level permits an audience to see patterns and the organization of parts. They can recognize hidden meanings and identify the components.

■ **Synthesis**—At this level, the audience can use old ideas to create new ones, generalize from given facts, relate knowledge from several areas, and predict or draw conclusions.

■ **Evaluation**—This is the highest level of learning, one at which audience members can compare and discriminate between ideas, and assess the value of theories and presentations. They make choices based on reasoned argument and verify the value of evidence. Astute learners also have the ability to recognize the presence of subjectivity at this level.

The attitude domain includes the way people deal with things emotionally, such as feelings, values, appreciation, enthusiasm, motivations, and opinions. The levels of learning in this domain range from the simplest human behavior to the most complex.

■ **Receiving**—This involves basic awareness, as well as a willingness to hear selected information. If you don't pay attention to something (perhaps because you don't understand it), you'll never come to appreciate it.

■ **Responding**—This level involves active participation on the part of the audience. They must listen and react to a particular phenomenon. Objectives might emphasize compliance or willingness to respond.

■ **Valuing**—This is about the worth or value a person attaches to a particular object, phenomenon, or behavior. This ranges from simple acceptance to the most complex state of commitment.

■ **Organizing**—Here, the audience can organize values into priorities by contrasting different values, resolving conflicts between them, and creating their own unique value system.

■ **Internalizing**—At this level, the audience has a value system that controls their behavior. The value system they have learned from your presentation is pervasive, consistent, predictable, and most importantly, characteristic of the individual learner.

What an audience *knows* about a subject may be very different from how they *feel* about it.

What do these categories mean for you as a speaker? Well, first, it indicates that what an audience *knows* about a subject may be very different from how they *feel* about it. Knowledge and attitude are entirely different issues for many people. If you talk to an audience about sailing, it's one thing to transfer information about the functions of a sail, a rudder, and the basic instruments of navigation; it's something entirely different if you convince them to enjoy sailing in rough weather. To accomplish that, you need to address their attitudes about the subject and convince them to confront and overcome their fears.

Knowing what you want your audience to learn from you is crucial to evaluating your success as a speaker. Making sure that your objectives are clearly defined and set at a level that's appropriate for your audience is equally important. You want to make certain that you're neither speaking above their heads nor insulting them with ideas and concepts that are too elementary for their level of understanding.

# TRUTH

7

## Talk is the work

Managers across all industries, according to consultant Deirdre Borden, spend about 75 percent of their time in verbal interaction. Those daily interactions include one-on-one dialogue, telephone conversations, videoconferencing, presentations to small groups, and—with increasing frequency—public speaking to larger audiences.

While an important fraction of a manager's work ends up in writing—notably the most important projects and ideas—much of the preparation for the decisions involved takes place orally. Managers transfer and acquire most of the information they need to do their jobs by speaking to one another. Most will tell you, in fact, that they don't leave a briefing to a group of colleagues to go back to their office to work. Those briefings, talks, and presentations *are* their work.

So, let's understand why managers speak. Often, you don't have a choice. As a manager, you'll occasionally find yourself preparing to speak on a topic you'd rather not discuss with a particular audience. Addressing the corporate executive committee on the subject of a quarterly budget shortfall is no one's idea of a good time, but you

> Managers transfer and acquire most of the information they need to do their jobs by speaking to one another.

do it because it's part of your management responsibility. You give many presentations because you are told to or because you must. Giving a talk in these situations isn't easy, but you certainly shouldn't be afraid to do so.

Many speaking opportunities, however, are voluntary in nature. Sometimes you give the talk because you choose to do so. You drop in on a group of employees to share the good news that the company has just landed a big contract they had worked hard to secure. You could have shared that information in an e-mail message or a memo, but you'd rather see their faces, hear them cheer, and watch them give each other "high fives" around the room.

On another occasion, you may explain to your daughter's elementary-school class what you do for a living. (Come to think of it, this might be tougher than the employee meeting.) You might also accept an invitation from a local Kiwanis club to speak at their weekly luncheon. Each speaking opportunity you accept and each speech you give will increase your self-assurance and reinforce your competence, confidence, and ability to speak well in public.

Every speaking opportunity, even an involuntary one, becomes an occasion for you to show what you know and to demonstrate your skills. Joan Finnessy, vice president of finance at Fisher Scientific International in Pittsburgh, Pennsylvania, found that out firsthand in a prior job:

> A few years ago, I was working as a division controller for a company that held a worldwide conference for its controllers. All the controllers in the company were required to make a presentation at this conference. Our company had recently purchased another organization, but we were not aware that the company was planning to reorganize itself and reduce the number of controllers.
>
> Senior managers were, of course, in attendance. We all had our few minutes "in the spotlight." Some controllers did a very good job at displaying strong delivery skills and solid content. Others did not do as well. They assumed the purpose of the presentations was to communicate information about our divisions for the benefit of others at the conference.
>
> Approximately a month later, however, those controllers who did not display good presentation skills found themselves in negotiations for severance packages.
>
> While nothing was ever said about a connection between poor presentations and terminations, only those individuals who did not present well were terminated.

Taking control of the situation and preparing yourself to succeed are the two keys to receiving a successful evaluation every time.

Even if you haven't been expressly told that you're being evaluated during a speech, one thing seems clear: You're being evaluated. Taking control of the situation and preparing yourself to succeed are the two keys to receiving a successful evaluation every time.

# TRUTH
## 8

# Know what your audience is looking for

There is nothing more important than your audience. Some speakers look at audience members as the enemy: They're the ones inducing stress in the speaker, they're the ones with the difficult questions, and they're the ones who are seemingly impossible to please.

The truth is, however, the audience is the only reason you're there. I talk later about analyzing your audience and getting to know them better. For now, let's concentrate on what they'll be looking for in your presentation.

Most audience members will tell you that they come to a presentation looking for something they can use that is positive and beneficial to them. The audience generally assesses that content in three ways: organization, expression, and support.

> **The audience is the only reason you're there.**

*Organization* is the simplest and easiest of the three criteria to explain. Your task is to organize your presentation in a way that makes sense to your audience. The better organized it is, the greater the chance they'll pay attention and do what you want. If you make *them* do the work, either because you're unable or unwilling to organize your thoughts, the audience won't like it. If they're highly motivated and know they'll receive some useful benefit from organizing the information you present, they may stay with you. They won't like it, but they'll stay engaged. If the reward doesn't justify the effort, though, they'll simply check out.

You can use any of these organizational patterns to make your presentation useful, interesting, and easy to understand.

- **Chronological Order**—Time is the controlling pattern here. Start at the beginning and move to the end. Or start with a particular event and move backward in time. Consistently provide time references in your presentation to hold the audience's attention.

- **Topical Organization**—When one issue is no more important than any other, you may want to organize your speech by topic, one after another.

- **Cause and Effect**—This type of organization is good if you hope to establish a likely outcome from a particular known cause or if you hope to trace the cause of a known event or effect.

- **Problem-Solution**—This pattern examines the nature of a problem, poses alternative solutions, and then weighs those solutions according to a set of values the speaker provides. Speeches using this pattern usually offer the listener a particular solution that you favor.

- **Geographic**—Compass points are the controlling motif here. The talk moves from east to west, north to south, or in some other readily identifiable direction.

- **Spatial**—When compass points are inappropriate, you may want to organize a talk from front-to-back, left-to-right, top-to-bottom, inside-to-outside, stem-to-stern, or other nongeographic pattern. This pattern of organization works well when you are required to describe a physical object or the arrangement of objects in a room, for example.

*Expression* refers to the way in which you deliver your message. This criterion encompasses the words you choose, the phrasing and pacing you employ, and the way you articulate your message. Your aim, remember, is to get the audience to like you and to buy into your message. The clearer and easier to understand your presentation is, the more likely your listeners will tune into what you're saying. The best way to communicate directly with your audience is to use words they understand. Using plain English in your speech will go a long way toward winning friends and influencing people.

Finally, *support* refers to the evidence that you offer to convince your audience of your line of reasoning. In addition to providing order and structure, and expressing yourself in ways that your listener will understand, you should consider the type and amount of evidence your audience will find convincing. This may include logic, emotion, appeals to authority, examples of others who've successfully used your ideas, or comments from people who are likely to influence the perceptions, thinking, and action of your audience.

# TRUTH

# 9

## There is a difference between speaking and writing

Before you decide to gather people in one room and speak to them, consider whether you really need to give a presentation. Alternative communication channels may be more useful, productive, and efficient. They may be less expensive, as well.

Think for a minute about the essential differences between speaking and writing: *Writing* produces a permanent record and can be used to convey great detail. It's often much more precise than a spoken presentation and can be used to carefully control wording. *Speaking*, on the other hand, produces a richer context, including nonverbal cues. It seems less rigid, less permanent, and may be more effective.

If you plan to gather a group of employees to hear about the implementation of a new business strategy, then a speech may be a good idea, but only if they have enough background information to understand what you're about to say and if personal contact with the audience will advance both the speaker's and the listeners' goals. A speech is certainly more expensive than an e-mail or a memo. Just divide the monthly compensation by the number of hours worked times the number of people in the room, and then add the costs for lost productivity and opportunity. Be sure to calculate transportation, room-use costs, refreshments, and other incidentals, as well. The cost of a presentation can quickly add up to much more than another communication channel will cost.

Writing in the form of a memo, letter, report, or proposal may be more efficient, cheaper, and more effective than a presentation, depending on the needs of the audience. How will they take in and process the information you're passing to them? Will they need high levels of detail or tabular data to understand your key points? Will they require charts, graphs, and illustrations? Will they want to read at their own pace and convenience and then return to the information for later reference?

A written document can take on a life of its own and is certainly more permanent than the spoken word. The choice you make depends on the needs of your audience and, frequently, the customs and culture of your business organization. At Procter & Gamble, brand managers aren't permitted to raise issues in team meetings unless their ideas (and data) are first circulated to all team members in memo format. The conversations that take place during team meetings follow a strict agenda, which is established during prior circulation of the memo.

Electronic mail may be a much more efficient channel, as well. It's certainly quicker than distributing documents on paper, and it's much easier to distribute an e-mail message than to disrupt people's schedules and get them together in a conference room or auditorium for a presentation. Keep in mind that e-mail is more like speaking than writing, though. The syntax, structure, and tone of e-mail are much closer to that of an oral conversation than they are to a written memo, letter, report, or proposal.

**A written document can take on a life of its own and is certainly more permanent than the spoken word. The choice you make depends on the needs of your audience and, frequently, the customs and culture of your business organization.**

Efficiency comes at a price, though. With quick, impromptu e-mail messages available at the convenience of the reader, you lose a great deal of texture and substance in your communications. For one thing, all of the nonverbal cues you regard as so important in a conversation or public speech are missing completely. Facial expressions, muscle tone, posture, arm and leg movement, and eye contact are gone. So are vocal cues such as pacing, phrasing, pitch, tone, timbre, forcefulness, volume, and more. You have a tough time distinguishing between sarcasm and criticism in e-mail because you can't hear the tone of the writer's voice. In the absence of other evidence, you're forced to accept what's written at face value.

A presentation or public speech, however, includes these nonverbal cues. No need to resort to cute little emoticons and smiley faces to convey the idea that you're just kidding. You can smile and deliver the message in a tone that tells your listeners you aren't actually serious. Most information exchanged in a human conversation, in fact, is transferred nonverbally. All of these cues are missing in a written document, but a speaker can take advantage of them when the audience is most receptive.

When Gordon Bethune was CEO of Continental Airlines, he recognized that a new strategy for reorganizing the airline would never work if he simply wrote it down in a memo or produced a slick brochure for his employees. They would need some advance information on his plans, of course, but he knew that he would have to meet with them in small groups and present his ideas personally. His sense of commitment, determination, and enthusiasm for the new plan would come across to Continental employees much more readily in person than it would on paper.

One further distinction between speaking and writing seems important. The spoken word handles large themes, big issues, and general trends quite nicely, but doesn't do nearly as well with detail. That's the reason you don't get much detail on the evening news about what happened in the stock market: "The Dow-Jones Industrials closed down more than seven points in mixed trading today on lighter-than-usual volume." But a newspaper account of this event would include a dozen paragraphs on what happened, along with stock tables and trend graphs. If detail is important to your listeners, then provide it to them in writing—either by directing them to the Internet or sending a downloadable PDF file, or by handing each member of the audience a report that provides the detail they expect and need.

> If detail is important to your listeners, then provide it to them in writing.

# TRUTH

# 10

# Preparing a presentation is a relatively simple process

The secret to creating a successful business presentation is preparation. While the process may seem daunting at first, it involves just 12 steps and a little determination.

1. **Select a topic**—While you clearly earn points for style in a business presentation, content is king. Substance matters and—repeat this to yourself, now—there is absolutely no substitute for knowing what you're talking about. This means, in every instance possible, that you should select a topic that's familiar to you so that you can talk knowingly on subjects you understand. Your audience will know instinctively whether you actually comprehend what you're saying, and they give high marks to experts who can make the subject matter come alive.

   > The secret to creating a successful business presentation is *preparation.*

2. **Analyze your audience**—It's all about them. They're the reason you're in the room; they're the reason you wrote the presentation. Get to know as much about them as possible. Knowledge of your audience is not a guarantee of success, but it's certainly a step in the right direction.

3. **Determine your purpose**—Know why you're speaking. If you aren't certain about this, then you shouldn't give a presentation. Understanding your role in the organization and in the lives of your listeners is especially important. This audience may want your views on the subject at hand and is keenly interested in your opinions. On the other hand, your purpose on a given day may be purely informative and the demand for your opinions may not be as brisk as you imagine.

4. **Learn what you can about the occasion**—Is your audience still in the fact-gathering stage or are they ready to make a decision? What's their reason for listening to you? How urgent is the matter you'll be speaking about? Are your listeners at the beginning or at the end of a process that will require them to take action of some sort? The more you learn about the context in which the presentation will take place, the more helpful you can be to the audience.

5. **Compose a thesis statement**—This is a one-sentence declaration of what you want the audience to know, understand, believe, or do. It should be brief, simple, and as complete as possible. Here's an example: "Company-supported carpooling will provide economic, operational, and environmental advantages to the firm." This thesis is direct, cogent, and offers a brief outline of your approach to the subject.

6. **Develop the main points**—You should cover only a few points, because you can never explain and support them all. The previous topic statement lends itself to a three-point pattern of support for your main contention and is relatively easy to follow. All of your evidence should relate to and support your principal reason for speaking.

7. **Gather supporting materials**—In addition to the main points, you also need actual evidence. Think about the kinds of proof that audience members find most convincing. You need to know something about them as individuals, as well as some sense of how much they already know about this subject. The support you gather should be compelling, recent, and fully transparent to your listeners. That is, they should know where you found your evidence and why you think it's believable.

8. **Separate the speech into its major parts**—Think about the introduction, body, and conclusion. Knowing what you plan to say, and in what order, will be helpful as you draft your outline. Think about the introduction and conclusion last, even though they may be the most memorable parts of your talk.

9. **Outline the speech**—A one-page outline of your remarks will prove helpful as you begin writing the presentation. Think about the issues you raise, the sequence in which you address each of them, and the evidence you offer your audience in support of those ideas. Once you know how to begin the talk, what main points to offer, and how to conclude your remarks, then you'll be ready to write.

10. **Consider presentation aids**—Visual support helps to explain, reinforce, and clarify your main points. If you can't *say* it easily, perhaps you can *show* it to your audience. Visuals tend to work best when you have new data; complex, technical information; or a new context for your subject.

39

11. **Write the speech**—Some speakers prefer to leave their remarks in cryptic, bullet-point format so that the speech takes on an extemporaneous tone. Others prefer to have each portion of the presentation written out, word for word, so they know exactly what they plan to say and in which order. Write in a way that best suits your speaking style, but remember that your listeners want to hear you speak to them, not read to them.

12. **Prepare your notes**—Some speakers use PowerPoint or presentation software as their memory prompt. Others use 3"-by-5" note cards to capture the essence of what they plan to say. Still others prefer to work from a full manuscript. I'll talk about this choice later, but keep in mind that your aim is to make the experience enjoyable, effortless, and interesting for the listener. Use a system of notes that is simple, easy to transport, and doesn't prevent you from maintaining eye contact with the audience.

# TRUTH

# 11

## Begin by analyzing your audience

Dartmouth business professor Mary Munter says that analyzing an audience involves answering four questions: (1) Who are they?; (2) What do they know?; (3) How do they feel?; and (4) How can you motivate them? If you can answer those, you are well on your way to crafting a presentation that's engaging, useful, and worth listening to.

**Who are they?** Audiences may be seen according to the roles or functions they play in the communication process. Your *primary audience* is composed of those who will receive your message directly. They're the folks in the room who are paying attention to what you say and what you show them. The *secondary audience* is that collection of people who will receive your message indirectly. They could be family, friends, co-workers, or associates of those in your primary audience. Consider who may be hidden from view as you speak to this particular group. Could a reporter hear about this from someone in the room? What about a competitor or a business partner? Knowing who is in the audience may be crucial to achieving your goals for the presentation.

**What do they know?** As you prepare for a presentation, ask yourself how much background information your audience will need. How much new information will they require to do what you ask of them? The more they know, the less you have to give them, provided that what they know is current, accurate, and relevant.

**What are their expectations and preferences?** Each audience has a preference for the style, channel, and format of a presentation. Even if they exhibit preferences similar to your own, it's still useful to know what they prefer. Do they like (or expect) a direct or indirect speaking style? That's mostly a cultural determination, of course; the vast majority of North American business managers say they prefer a direct approach: Tell me what you want, then support the request. Reveal up front what your purpose is and what you expect of the audience. Only when you know (or suspect) the audience disagrees with you should you delay revealing your rhetorical purpose. Communicate with an audience in its preferred style and format and they'll reward you with their time and attention.

**How do they feel about this?** It's helpful to know the audience's level of interest in your message. If it's not particularly high, you may have to provide additional motivation for them to care. What's their probable bias: positive, negative, or neutral? You can work with an audience that's hostile to your viewpoint, but you have to go about it carefully, building agreement and concurrence as you go. Finally, will this be relatively easy for them to buy into or somewhat difficult? The closer your message is to the center of their comfort zone, the easier it is to secure their agreement.

**How can you motivate them?** Each of us is driven, in general, by somewhat different motives. We each have different interests, needs, and levels of satisfaction that affect how we respond to a speaker's appeal. Broadly speaking, four categories of evidence may prove useful to you when preparing your presentation.

1.  **Shared values** may provide a way for you to establish common ground with your audience. Begin with views and values you hold in common and then move on to topics where disagreement is more likely.

2.  **Basic needs** form the most fundamental appeal for a speaker. These needs might range from the basics of existence to relatedness needs and growth needs.

3.  **Rationality and consistency** will appeal to the desire of your audience members to act in consistent, rational, and sensible ways. If you can show that what you want from them is entirely consistent with what they already believe or the ways in which they already live, then you have a good chance of securing their acceptance and agreement.

4.  **Social conformity** is a powerful motivator. Most people want to fit it with their peer groups and be seen as cooperative, collaborative, and helpful to others. Admired individuals, such as parents, teachers, celebrities, and others can help set the pace. Peer groups exert powerful influence on each of us, as do social norms and societal expectations. The truth is, we all just want to fit in somehow, and particularly with those we admire most.

You really can never know too much about your audience, even if you're convinced you know them well. The better you understand their collective mindset, concerns, and motivations, the greater your chances for success with them.

# TRUTH
# 12

## Know your audience

Who are these people? What do you know about them? What do they know about you or your subject? Before you go any further in your preparation, ask a few simple questions about the people in your audience. Once you know more about them, you can figure out how to motivate them to listen. These categories of information might prove useful as you prepare your remarks.

**Age**—How old are your audience members? Will they be familiar with the concepts you plan to speak about? What's their vocabulary range? What sort of life experiences have they had? Remember, if you're speaking to a group of twenty-year-olds, you know that they were born in the latter years of the second Reagan administration. They have no direct memory of the Berlin Wall coming down. Saddam Hussein invaded Kuwait while these folks were in kindergarten. And Bill Clinton was elected President when they were in second grade. Make certain your references to events and ideas are both known to them and relevant to their concerns. Similarly, an older audience might have been around for certain events, but references to Napster, MySpace, MP3s, or an episode of "Aqua Teen Hunger Force" may well be lost on them.

> Before you go any further in your preparation, ask a few simple questions about the people in your audience. Once you know more about them, you can figure out how to motivate them to listen.

**Education**—Knowing the age of the audience tells you something about how much education they have had, but perhaps not as much as you would like to know. Presentation content, including central themes and vocabulary, is certainly influenced by the level and type of education of your audience.

**Personal beliefs**—Knowing what this group believes may well be more important than knowing their age or education level. The reason is simple: Your beliefs define who you are. Are these folks liberal or conservative? What's their political affiliation? Are they committed to a particular religious or social point of view? Do they have certain biases favoring or opposing such issues as red meat, cigar smoking, gun ownership, or parallel parking?

**Occupation**—What do these people do for a living? Are they students? As such, many of them may not work for a living but might hope to have occupations someday. Are they managers, professionals, or colleagues of yours? Knowing how people earn their living will tell you something about their educational background and daily routines, as well as their motivations and interests.

**Socioeconomic status**—This term describes where in the social/economic spectrum your audience is located. And it is, of course, a direct function of other factors such as income, education, occupation, neighborhood, friends, family, and more. Think of this as a single descriptor that explains just how much prestige your audience has in the eyes of others in society.

**Ethnic origin**—This may be worthwhile to know, but its value is limited. The utility of this information lies in knowing which issues and positions are of greatest concern to members of a particular ethnic group. The limitation lies in knowing that you cannot reasonably stereotype the views of all members of such a group. Sensitivity to ethnic causes and issues, as well as language, should be sufficient as you prepare a speech.

**Gender**—Considerable evidence now indicates that this may be among the least useful pieces of information you might want to know about your audience. Why? Because study after study shows no statistically significant difference in the responses of professional men and women to a wide range of stimuli. Clearly, knowing that your audience is composed exclusively of one sex or another might alter your approach, but writing one speech for men and another for women is unwise. Treat the audience as intelligent humans, and you will get the response you're seeking.

**Knowledge of the subject**—This may be the one category of information (along with the next) that you would be willing to buy to know more about your audience. A thorough knowledge of what your audience already knows about your speaking subject is useful in a number of ways. First, this information tells you where to begin. Don't patronize them by explaining fundamentals they already understand.

Similarly, don't start talking above their heads. Begin at a point they're comfortable with and move on from there.

**Attitudes toward the subject**—Even more important than what they know about your subject is how they feel about it. What I know about the federal tax code is far less relevant than how I feel about it when I listen to a talk about tax reform. My emotions are not irrelevant as I approach a subject. Neither are yours. And you certainly should anticipate what the emotional response of your audience will be to the content and direction of your talk. The greater the degree of *ego involvement* (or emotional response) to a given topic, the narrower the range of acceptable positions. In other words, people are much more open-minded on topics they are indifferent to than they are on topics they care about passionately. What you don't know in this regard *can* hurt you.

# TRUTH

## 13

# Understand what makes people listen

If a presentation is a learning occasion for the audience, it's also a listening occasion. It's an opportunity for them to hear, tune into, and make sense of what's being said. But listening is hard work. Listening involves intellectual and physical effort on the part of the listener and, unless properly motivated, is something most people would rather not do.

So, how *do* you get an audience to listen? As it happens, people listen to a presenter for three principal reasons: self-interest, who's telling it, and how it's told.

Many audience members arrive at a presentation with personal interests that serve as powerful motivators to listen. Some of those whom you'll speak to, in fact, are actively seeking information on the subject of your speech. They're interested, enthusiastic, and eager to hear what you have to say.

> People listen to a presenter for three principal reasons: self-interest, who's telling it, and how it's told.

Others, not so much. They're in the room because they're told to be there, because someone else more interesting to them is speaking after you, or because they have no other engagements at that time. A small fraction of the audience honestly couldn't care less—They see this as just another opportunity to get away from the office or avoid doing real work.

Sometimes, an audience is attracted to a presentation simply because of the speaker. The subject of the talk doesn't matter to many of them; it's the speaker they've come to hear. Celebrities often draw a crowd due to name recognition alone. Oprah Winfrey, Jack Welch, and Al Gore can easily fill an auditorium with eager listeners without ever publishing the title of their talks. A lesser-known speaker, on the other hand, has the uphill task of drawing a crowd based on the actual content of the presentation.

Then there is the issue of how it's told. Audiences are, in many important ways, much the same the world over. At the very least, they want something worthwhile in exchange for their time; they want to feel as if the effort and energy they invest in paying attention to and trying to make sense of a presentation is worth it. Most people want more, though. They want entertainment. They want to feel amused, captivated, excited, inspired, thrilled, and more. That's asking a lot of a public speech.

So, how can you make the experience of listening to you worthwhile? The simple answer is reward the audience for their efforts. You certainly don't have control over their self-interests. Even though you may have done a substantial amount of research about the people in your audience, you're still unlikely to know them all. Knowing what motivates each of them to listen, learn, and act on what they've heard is all but impossible.

The idea that your name will draw a crowd is equally unlikely. Perhaps, after reading this book and working on your presentation skills, you can make a name for yourself and develop the sort of reputation that can pack an auditorium. But that's still in the future. What you do have control over is how the message is delivered.

You (probably) have control over the topic you choose to speak on, the organizational pattern you develop, and the evidence you select to support your main points. You also determine how you

> What you do have control over is how the message is delivered.

introduce the subject, the forms of motivation you offer the audience, and the structure of the ideas you present to them. You're also in charge of delivery, and that includes the rate at which you speak, when and where you choose to pause, how loudly you speak, the tone and pitch of your voice, and how well you project your voice into the room. You're in control of the gestures and body language you use, and that includes everything from posture to eye contact. You regulate the length of the talk, the development of ideas, the introduction of evidence, and the number of times you repeat yourself. These issues associated with how the story is told are all well within your control. You're not dependent on the audience to arrive with a special interest in your subject, nor do you need advance publicity to influence the outcome. It's all within your grasp and, believe me, the audience knows if you're good at this and they can reward you.

If the people seated before you have invested their time and energy (and perhaps some money) in attending your talk, the least you can do is make it worth their while.

# TRUTH

14

## Your speaking style makes a difference

Among the factors that quickly influence whether an audience wants to listen to you is your speaking style. You have to develop your own style through practice, experience, and by watching and listening to others.

New York-based communication consultant Sonya Hamlin asked a number of people, including business managers, friends, and associates, about their reactions to various speaking styles. She compiled an impressive list of stylistic elements that are positive, as well as those that are negative.

Hamlin found that people react positively to speakers who are *warm, friendly, and interesting*. What does warm mean? While that's a bit hard to define, most people certainly can tell if people are "warm" on meeting them. In the autumn of 1960, when John F. Kennedy was running for president against Richard Nixon, the two candidates agreed to a televised debate that would showcase each man's ideas, intellect, and rhetorical skills.

The debate was broadcast on both television and radio. Surprisingly, judging who won seemed to depend directly on whether you saw the debate on television or heard it on the radio. A scientific survey of people who tuned into the debate revealed

## People react positively to speakers who are *warm, friendly, and interesting.*

that those who only listened to the exchange thought Richard Nixon had won. He answered the questions in detail, had good debating points, was specific about his policies and proposals, and seemed in command of the facts. People who saw the debate on television thought Jack Kennedy had won—hands down. Even though Kennedy evaded a number of questions and sidestepped some difficult issues, people were impressed with his demeanor, presence, and charisma. In a word, they thought he was *warm*.

Audiences also like listening to people who are *organized and confident*. Organization helps, of course, because it's one more thing listeners won't have to do for themselves. And confidence wins friends. If you're not confident about a subject, then why should the audience give you their attention? If you show them your enthusiasm, they will reward you with their undivided attention.

Another positive speaking style includes speakers who are *open, honest, and authentic.* Keep in mind that stylistic preferences are based on cultural norms, so these ideas apply primarily to North American audiences. They really seem to like people who step out from behind the podium to show that they are open to questions, criticism, and the views of the audience. And most audiences universally respect speakers who are not only honest with them, but also are who they appear to be.

They also like speakers who are *knowledgeable, creative, and inspiring.* They've come to learn something and want to know what you know about this subject. They're keen to know whether you have any useful insights on the topic and if you can inspire them to listen, learn, and do more with the subject at hand.

Hamlin also identified a number of negative speaking styles that can turn off an audience. Most North American audiences don't care for speakers who are *pompous, patronizing, stuffy, or exceedingly formal.* Audiences also react negatively to speakers who are *vague, complex, and unsure of themselves.* Again, the spoken word is not a medium that handles detail well. The greater the level of complexity in a speech, the more likely an audience will become confused, bored, or disinterested.

Finally, audiences are often dismissive of speakers who are *irrelevant, monotonous, or nervous.* Relevance, of course, is all about their interests. If you can make your talk relevant to the audience and their needs, they'll tune in and pay attention. They won't listen to a monotone delivery or to a speaker who displays unusual levels of nervousness. When former senator John Edwards began his campaign for the Democratic presidential nomination in 2007, people who gathered to hear him in fire halls, community centers, and cafes came away with a similar reaction to his presentations: "He seems so comfortable, so natural, and so much at ease in front of a crowd." Edwards developed this style through many years of working as a lawyer, trying to win the hearts and minds of people in a courtroom jury box, and it's particularly effective in politics.

The way you choose to approach your subject and the occasion, and your knowledge of the audience will greatly influence their reaction to you.

So, think about your speaking style. The way you choose to approach your subject and the occasion, and your knowledge of the audience will greatly influence their reaction to you. Work to develop a positive style that captivates your listeners and, at the same time, try to eliminate the negative, problematic elements that drive them away.

# 15

Anticipate the questions
your audience brings to your
presentation

As listeners arrive in a conference room, lecture hall, or auditorium, they already have questions in mind about the topic. They have other concerns, as well: Will this be painful or pleasant? Will I learn anything today? Is any of this going to be useful or will it simply be a waste of time? In addition to the usual anxieties people have about attending a presentation, most audiences will have the following kinds of questions about the speaker, as well.

**Do you know what I need to know?**   As the audience sizes you up, your task is to convince them that you know something they either want or need to know. You should state your credentials or experience in the introduction and give a brief overview of your talk. If you can show them what you know, up front, they may pay attention long enough to learn something.

**Can I trust you?**   People will trust someone they believe, as well as someone they respect and think is fair. Borrowing credibility from others as you begin is often a good way to establish your trustworthiness. This is most easily done by arranging for someone the audience trusts to introduce you.

**Am I comfortable with you?**   If you make the audience nervous or uncomfortable during your speech, then they aren't going to learn much. If they aren't having fun or don't want to be in the room with you, you'll have little chance of influencing them in a meaningful way. Demonstrating that you're at ease and comfortable with the audience, topic, and occasion are ways to generate comfort among your listeners. Don't ever tell them you're nervous or display anxiety that might reveal how unhappy you are about the prospect of speaking to them.

**How can you affect me?**   During a presentation, people want to know how you will affect them and the lives they're leading. Will you be helpful or instructive? Are you supportive of their goals and ambitions? If you can show the audience how the content of your talk will have a beneficial effect on them, you'll get their attention. Negative messages are necessary

> People want to know how you will affect them and the lives they're leading.

from time to time, but if you can demonstrate the value or benefit of what you're saying, you'll keep the audience with you. One of their greatest concerns as a presentation begins is that the topic will be completely irrelevant to them.

**If you can demonstrate the value or benefit of what you're saying, you'll keep the audience with you.**

**What's my experience with you?**   Your credibility is also an issue here. Your integrity is based, in part, on who you are and who you represent, but it's also based on the audience's prior experience with you. If you've given them any reason to distrust you in the past, you'll have to work hard to overcome that. If their previous experience with you was positive, then they will trust you and it will be easier to influence this group. Of course, if they have no idea who you are, then you'll have to work to establish your sincerity and credibility from the moment you begin speaking. A speech that focuses on shared values frequently works well under such circumstances.

**Are you reasonable?**   Audience members want to know if what you're asking of them is reasonable. Not rational or logical, but within reason. Are your ideas and proposals within their comfort zone? If what you want from them falls outside or near the edges of their comfort zone, you'll have a hard time winning them over. You can often show an audience that your ideas are reasonable by offering an endorsement from someone they respect or admire. If no endorsements are available, you might try a respected public figure or expert who is in agreement with you. In the end, your task is to convince them that what you want is both reasonable and perfectly natural. Dealing with common fears and objections is a technique that gets an audience to acknowledge barriers to acceptance and often shows them how irrational or unreasonable those fears are. If you don't deal with the issues they're afraid of, you'll never win their hearts and minds, because people will act more swiftly and completely on their fears than they ever will on their hopes and dreams.

Acknowledging that every audience has concerns, anxieties, and questions is a big first step toward getting them to accept you and buy into your message. However, if the answers to the half-dozen questions you've just considered are mostly negative, you'll never get what you want from the audience.

# TRUTH

# 16

## Listening matters

You understand how valuable communication is to the success of any business. And you also understand the value of skillful communication on a personal level. You make friends, establish relationships, pass ideas, and accomplish the work that earns your living each day. Yet, strangely, the communication skill most central to your success in life is the one you're least likely to study in a formal way: listening.

Recent studies show that more than half of an adult's daily conversations are spent listening to someone else speak. Even though listening is clearly a crucial skill, few people know how to do so efficiently and effectively. Professor Ralph Nichols of the University of Minnesota warns us, however, that "...listening is hard work. It is characterized by faster heart action, quicker circulation of the blood, a small rise in bodily temperature." The implication is simple: If you are not motivated to work at listening, you are not likely to improve this skill.

Studies of listening skill repeatedly show that the average North American adult listens at an efficiency rate of just 25 percent. Your mother was right: For most people, literally three-quarters of what you hear goes in one ear and out the other. You retain and understand just a fraction of what's going on around you.

> More than half of an adult's daily conversations are spent listening to someone else speak.

There is a substantial difference, though, between hearing and listening. On the one hand, hearing is merely an involuntary physical response to the environment. Listening, on the other hand, is a process that includes hearing, attending to, understanding, evaluating, and responding to spoken messages. It's a sophisticated communication skill that can be mastered only with considerable practice. And though improving one's listening skills is difficult, demanding, and challenging, it is also immensely rewarding.

Why have most of us become so resistant to careful listening? "It's because of our fast-paced world," says Kathy Thompson of Alverno

College. "We're always in a hurry. Mentally we're saying, 'Get to the point.' We don't have time to hear the whole story. We're running from house to job to store to church. Good listening takes time."

That's part of it, according to Wick Chambers, a partner in Speechworks, a communications-training firm. "But also, people think listening is boring; it's more fun to talk." Still others blame television and radio, which allow people to combine listening with so many other activities that listening to only one thing—to music, for example—seems like a waste of time.

"When you watch television," says Sheila Bentley, a communications consultant, "you're listening in a way that doesn't require you to retain anything and doesn't object if you leave the room. And because it's interrupted by commercials, you don't have to develop sustained attending skills. With people spending six hours a day doing that kind of listening, it's no wonder there's concern that we're becoming a nation of poor listeners."

Poor listening can cause disasters, as it did in the 1977 runway collision at Tenerife Airport in the Canary Islands, when misunderstood instructions caused 583 deaths. But more often, poor listening results in hundreds of little, time-wasting mistakes a day—the wrong coffee order, credit card charge, or telephone number.

At Starbucks coffee stores, where a customer can order a "double-shot decaf grande iced half-skim vanilla dry cappuccino," employees are taught a procedure for listening to and calling out orders developed by the company five years ago. It systematizes the sequence of words

**Poor listening results in hundreds of little, time-wasting mistakes a day.**

describing the drink—size, flavoring, milk, decaf—with automatic defaults. Then the person making the drink echoes the order aloud. "We expect our employees to listen," says Alan Gulick, a Starbucks spokesman. "It's an important component of customer service."

Listening is the central skill used in establishing and maintaining relationships. No matter what type of relationship—professional, personal, neighborly, romantic—listening is the skill that forms the bond and keeps the relationship moving forward. Harvard psychologist Daniel Goleman says, "Listening is a skill that keeps couples together. Even in the heat of an argument, when both are seized by emotional hijacking, one or the other, and sometimes both, can manage to listen past the anger, and hear and respond to a partner's reparative gesture."

# 17

## Being an active listener brings real benefits

Being an active listener can enhance your life in numerous ways. Both academic and business-related research show that good listening skills provide various benefits, including increased knowledge, job success, improved personal relationships, and self-protection, among others.

Studies of human behavior have shown a steady tendency during the last fifty years in the United States toward more passive learning techniques and more passive leisure activities. As a society, Americans spend more time watching television, movies, and videos, and less time reading. Coincidentally, we also spend more time these days listening to CDs, tapes, and the radio.

**Good listening skills provide various benefits, including increased knowledge, job success, improved personal relationships, and self-protection.**

A 1981 study conducted by Unisys Corporation reported that students spend 60 to 70 percent of their time in a classroom listening. Professors Ralph Nichols and Leonard Stevens found in their studies at the University of Minnesota that every group of students receiving instruction in listening improved by at least 25 percent, while some groups improved by as much as 40 percent. Without some instruction in listening improvement, however, it appears that the listening abilities of most people actually decline from elementary school on.

In addition to these findings, a number of other good reasons exist for you to improve your listening skills:

**Listening demonstrates acceptance**—The very act of listening to another person demonstrates that you value him and care about what he is saying. If you show that you *don't care* about others, they'll stop talking to you. Good, perhaps, in the short run, but disastrous in the long run.

**Listening promotes problem-solving abilities**—Leaders, parents, and managers are often asked to do what bartenders, cab drivers, and counselors have done for years: give someone the time (and attention) to talk through a problem. Rather than providing advice and solutions right away, most successful managers encourage employees to arrive at solutions on their own. By listening carefully and reflectively, you can guide someone else to find a solution that has a greater chance for success and substantially greater levels of acceptance than if you provided the answer.

**Listening increases the speaker's receptiveness to the thoughts and ideas of others**—The best ideas don't always come from yourself or your immediate staff and colleagues. Often, you'll find great ideas where you least expect them. They may come from your customers, your employees, your suppliers and business partners, and (interestingly) from people who elected not to do business with you. You might be genuinely surprised at what your competitor's customers are saying about you, if only you'd take the time to listen to them.

**Listening increases the self-esteem of the other person**—You are not personally responsible for everyone else's self-esteem, but think about it for a moment. Isn't it easier to come to work, concentrate on the tasks at hand, and compete successfully if you feel good about yourself? Sales managers have known for years that self-esteem is crucial to a sales representative's ability to succeed. They hear "no" so often from potential clients that they come to accept failure as an inevitable part of the job. Anyone who's raised small children will tell you the same thing. Having a friend who'll listen willingly and uncritically can be enormously helpful.

**Listening helps to prevent head-on emotional collisions**—If you concentrate on your own needs to the exclusion of other people's needs and interests, you will find that others will return the favor: They will focus on their own interests and not yours. The key to preventing the sort of emotional train wrecks that are destructive to any organization is to put other people's needs ahead of your own. Listen to their concerns and interests *first*, and you will likely get what you want from them sooner and with substantially less angst.

By taking responsibility for successful communication through active and reflective listening, you can become more successful at those activities that depend on good communication, in both your personal and professional life. Being a better listener helps make you a better presenter because you've taken the time to find out what's on the minds of those who'll be listening to you. Good listening skills help you to learn more, improve your relationships with others, and increase your chances for success. Careful listening is no guarantee, of course, but it's a wonderful place to start.

# TRUTH

# 18

## You can overcome the barriers to successful communication

Every presenter faces potential barriers to success as a speaking occasion arises. Some barriers are fairly mundane: Am I available that evening? Can I reschedule another obligation? Will I be able to gather the information I need to answer their questions? Other barriers, though, are more serious and can present great difficulties for a speaker. Obstacles to success appear to fall broadly into five categories:

**Stereotypes**—Stereotyping is to ascribe to all members of a group or class those characteristics or behaviors observed in just one or a few. The word was coined by social scientist Walter Lippmann in 1921 when he wrote about why people so readily imagine how other people are, or why they behave as they do, even in the face of ready evidence to the contrary. The fact is people are comfortable with stereotypes. They help to explain the world around you, don't require much effort to construct, and give you categories into which you can insert new experiences, new people, and new ideas. Treating each person as unique or different is much more difficult and requires a great deal more reasoning and work on your part. Stereotypes may be useful as a starting point from which to understand groups and their members, but they can be very damaging when you fail to acknowledge differences within those groups or when you fail to admit that not all people act or think in the same ways.

**Prejudice**—This is a word derived from Latin, meaning "to judge before knowing." You do it all the time. In fact, it's not necessarily bad. You have little prejudices that serve you well: the food you eat, the stores you shop in, your taste in clothing. Often, when you speak, you are forced to judge before you have all the facts. You simply don't have the time or the resources to gather more information. You must act now.

As you speak to others, though, it's best to acknowledge that you are working with incomplete data. Admit that you don't know as much as you might like, or, perhaps, that you simply didn't have time to gather information that might have been easily available to you. You don't want others making judgments about you too quickly.

> You don't want others making judgments about you too quickly.

The best way to encourage that sort of careful thinking in others is to lead by example and admit to your prejudicial thinking whenever possible.

**Feelings**—Keep your emotions in check. Control your anger. Don't display your contempt for others and their ideas in public. This is all good advice, but it's easier said than done. Your emotions and those of your audience can easily get in the way of an objective look at the facts. These feelings can blur the important distinctions that exist between factual data and your interpretation of what they mean.

> Your emotions and those of your audience can easily get in the way of an objective look at the facts.

The best advice is simply to acknowledge that you have feelings and then use them to advance your cause. You must also recognize, however, that the people in your audience will have feelings— about you, your subject, and your evidence—and those feelings may be at odds with your own. Acknowledge that and then move on to make your case as best you can.

**Language**—You probably know from a basic communication course that words don't have meaning, people do. People assign meaning to the words they hear and read, and people with different backgrounds, different educations, and different life experiences will assign much different meanings to the words you speak. This will happen during the course of a single speech. Various audience members will hear the same words at precisely the same moment, spoken by the same person, yet they will assign different meaning to those words and leave the speech with different impressions of what the speaker meant.

Work around the difficulties inherent in interpreting language by offering multiple examples to illustrate your key points. Often a graph, table, or visual display conveys more meaning than whole paragraphs. Give your audience several ways to understand what you mean: Repeat yourself, rephrase your intentions, tell stories, and give examples.

**Culture**—No two people are the same, not only because of genetic individual differences, but also because each one has been raised in different ways. We tend to think of culture as an expression of entire nations or civilizations, but it's really much more specific than that. You have various experiences as you grow up, become educated, find your life's work, and live out your lives. The experiences of one generation are not the same as those of another. Customs, habits, and preferences in food and music are different from one ethnic group to another. And if you look carefully, you can see the cultural differences that exist among various corporations and business organizations. Some have a preference for informality while others prefer more structure. Various habits, from the use of titles to the use of time, distinguish one group from another. Your response to the cultural habits and preferences of others is a mark of your respect for them and an acknowledgment that they are not only different, but also that those differences are important to them.

Keep in mind that communication obstacles can provoke negative reactions. When people feel threatened, intimidated, lost, or confused, a number of things can happen. If the audience experiences these feelings during a speech, they may stop listening. They may discover how much they don't know, which can lead to frustration, anger, and hostility toward the speaker and the ideas being discussed. If the speaker makes them feel sufficiently dumb, they may withdraw entirely.

Start with what the audience already knows and then move on to ideas that are a logical extension or outcome of those they are familiar with.

When giving a presentation, begin with the familiar and move to the unfamiliar. Start with what the audience already knows and then move on to ideas that are a logical extension or outcome of those they are familiar with. Don't intimidate or confuse your audience. Do everything you can to make them feel that they are just as smart as you are. The reward, once again, is their attention and their willingness to think about your ideas.

# Develop support for your presentation

While your reputation or the topic of your presentation may keep an audience with you for a while, you have a better chance of convincing them of the value in your ideas if you support your talk with current, believable, easy-to-understand evidence.

Where should you begin? Well, starting with your own experience, knowledge, and interests is probably best. If you are genuinely interested in the ideas you plan to present, your audience will pick up on that and respond accordingly. You also know where to look for the most interesting, most believable support. If you like a particular subject, chances are good that you know which publications to read, know which experts are cited most often, and know a great deal about the latest developments. The confidence that comes with knowing all of this information will not be lost on your audience.

Second, consider new ideas, information, and techniques. You and your audience may together know a great deal about the subject of your talk, but your listeners may not know about the very latest information. That's where your interests can help them. Bring them up-to-date on the subject and share the latest innovations and developments.

Next, as you consider how to support your speech, think about the availability and quality of support material. You may have a special topic that you simply can't support because you will not have access to the right information by the time you must speak.

> Bring them up-to-date on the subject and share the latest innovations and developments.

Talk to some experts. Not all credible evidence is found in books, magazines, journals, newspapers, or on the Internet. Some of the most interesting and compelling evidence is testimony from people who are genuine experts on the subject. Where can you find them? They're all around you. A punch-press operator working on a factory floor may not seem like an expert, but if he's been at his job for a number of years, chances are good that he knows a great deal about the machinery, materials, and processes involved in the job. Ask him a few questions. You might be surprised how much you can learn if you listen carefully.

Know how much time is allotted for your speech. You can't include large amounts of detail if you have only a few minutes to speak. Because you know you must respect the time limits imposed on your talk, consider carefully how much information and the level of detail you'll have time to include. You'll have some idea of whether you need more or less information once you rehearse the speech. As you begin, of course, it's always better to have too much than too little evidence. You can easily edit a speech later; going back and beginning your research again as the speaking date approaches is much tougher.

Finally, think about the specific forms of evidence you plan to include in your presentation. This evidence comes in three general forms: logic, emotion, and source credibility. *Logic* refers to a system of reasoning used to derive sound conclusions from various premises. Behavioral psychologists have found that about three-quarters of all men and one-third of all women prefer to make decisions based on logic. They are rational, analytic, linear decision makers for whom logic makes great sense.

Not all people think in this way, however. About two-thirds of all women and one-quarter of all men prefer to make decisions based on emotion. They take human consequences into consideration as they gather evidence and think about what to do. They ask whose life goals are supported and what the outcomes are for the people involved. *Emotion* may be transitory and fleeting in nature, but it is very powerful as a means of motivating people to adopt a position and take action.

**Evidence comes in three general forms: logic, emotion, and source credibility.**

Finally, the *credibility* of the source itself matters to just about everyone. As you look at the evidence offered in a presentation, you take into consideration not only who's saying it, but also where the evidence originated. Revealing the source of your proof, relying on known and respected experts, and bolstering your viewpoint with statements of approval from people the audience admires is helpful in getting them to accept what you say.

# TRUTH

## 20

# Understand the power of
# your content

After making some judgments about the occasion, the topic on which you're speaking, and you as a speaker, your audience will turn their attention to the actual content of your speech. That content is heavily influenced by your purpose. As you've seen, different audience members react in varying ways to different kinds of evidence, so the material you select should not only reflect your purpose and the psychological needs of the audience, but it should also accurately and honestly reflect the subject itself. Your content will generally fall into several of these categories:

**Descriptions and explanations**—Objects are typically described, while processes and ideas are explained. If you give a talk on owning an iPod, for example, you first may have to describe what a digital music player is and how it works, followed by an explanation of how to download music selections from the Internet and store them on your hard drive or your music player. Providing visual reinforcement is always helpful as you describe and explain your topic, but your most powerful ally in reaching the audience is clear and accurate language.

**Comparisons and contrasts**— A comparison shows similarities between something known to the audience and something new that is introduced to them. Contrast, on the other hand, attempts to make a topic or point clear by showing how it differs from some other concept that is familiar to the audience.

> Your most powerful ally in reaching the audience is clear and accurate language.

**Examples, illustrations, and anecdotes**—These are common forms of amplification that are only slightly different from one another. In a recent commencement address, Xerox Corporation's chairman and CEO, Anne Mulcahy, cited examples of ethical failures among business leaders in support of her contention that executives should be more focused on servant leadership than personal achievement. In one anecdote about her promotion to the top job at Xerox, Mulcahy told the story of her decision to refund money taken by a predecessor from the employee retirement fund. That decision won her numerous fans among Xerox employees and retirees but very few friends on Wall Street, as it involved a significant charge against earnings. She did it because she honestly believed it was the right thing to do.

**Definitions**—Defining a word doesn't always mean using a dictionary entry. You can explain what you mean by tracing the origins of a word, by giving examples, by classifying the term in a category that's well known to the audience, or by explaining the function or purpose of the idea. "Insider trading," for example, is a term that most investors have heard and usually associate with illegal conduct. But the term actually includes both legal and illegal conduct. The legal version is when corporate insiders— officers, directors, and employees—buy and sell stock in their own companies.

**Statistics**—While some social scientists will tell you that a *statistic* is a characteristic of a sample and a parameter is a characteristic of a population, that's not how most people use these terms. In a presentation, statistics are actually quantified examples. Percentages and fractions are two of the quickest and easiest ways to make comparisons. For example, "The IRS estimates that unpaid taxes from individuals make up 70 percent of the tax shortfall each year." The important rule about using statistics is this: The figures you cite must be not only accurate, but they must fairly and honestly reflect the circumstance you're trying to describe.

**Testimonies**—Examples, illustrations, and statistics are ways of presenting an audience with factual, observable, and verifiable data. *Testimonies* establish facts secondhand, as when a witness tells what she saw at the scene of an accident. Testimonies are useful in providing opinions on matters where facts are not available. The credibility of the statements, however, rises or falls on the personal and professional credibility of the witnesses, so establish that beforehand by identifying and qualifying your sources.

> The figures you cite must be not only accurate, but they must fairly and honestly reflect the circumstance you're trying to describe.

**Quotations**—These are really a broader form of testimony. A direct quote can come from any number of sources and is often useful because of the credibility of the person you're quoting. A quote is used for any number of reasons—to establish context, to define an issue, or to inject humor into a speech—but what all useful quotes have in common is that they directly support the principal point you're trying to make. You needn't say "quote," "unquote" when you provide a quotation; you just need to make sure your audience understands that these are someone else's words and not yours. You should explain when and under what circumstances the quotation was first spoken.

**Repetition and restatement**—Repetition is among the most powerful tools available to a speaker. May I say that again? Repetition is among the most powerful tools available to a speaker. You can emphasize and enhance an idea simply by saying it again. Or you can restate it in similar but nonidentical terms. The fact is not everyone in your audience is paying attention at any given moment. If you repeat something you've said earlier or something you believe is particularly important, you reinforce those who've heard it already, and you catch the inattentive with your message for the first time.

> Repetition is among the most powerful tools available to a speaker.

# TRUTH

## 21

# The kinds and quality of evidence matter to your audience

81

The support you plan to include in your presentation comes in two basic forms. The first type is factual data in the form of examples or statistics. The second is testimonial evidence or statements of opinion about what is, has been, or is likely to be true in the future. Testimonial evidence is frequently used when a speaker has no factual basis available for judgment. It's needed when the presenter wants to make a prediction about what will happen in the future as a result of taking some current action.

Let's begin by considering testimonial evidence. The quality of factual and opinion evidence is best judged by the characteristics of the source of the testimony. There are several ways in which you can gauge the reliability of a source:

**Objectivity and accuracy record**—Some sources have a reputation for objectivity and accuracy, while others do not. Government agencies, such as the Census Bureau and the Department of Labor Statistics, for example, are generally considered to have a good record for providing accurate, unbiased information. The executive branch of the government doesn't have such a good record. Political appointees in this branch often release information that has an ideological or political bias—and this is true of both parties, really—to help achieve political objectives. *The Wall Street Journal* is considered more accurate and, at least on the news pages, more objective than, say, the *National Enquirer*.

> The quality of factual and opinion evidence is best judged by the characteristics of the source of the testimony.

**Expertise and knowledge of facts**—In the case of opinion evidence, a person's expertise and experience in a field are crucial. In fields such as criminology, medicine, economics, foreign affairs, or archaeology, the opinions of people with appropriate education and experience are generally trusted over those of a lay person or nonexpert. However, keep two key points in mind. First, expertise is subject-specific. Just because your dentist knows something about root canals and gingivitis doesn't mean he knows anything about the stock market. Second, even lay persons without any special forms of expertise may be just as reliable as an expert when reporting observed facts.

**Consistency**—This test has two aspects. The first is internal consistency; for example, does a particular source contradict itself in reports spread over an extended period of time or within the same report? The second aspect is that the information given by a source should be consistent with other sources. If not, then someone is mistaken and the evidence will have to be confirmed in some verifiable way before it's considered reliable.

Now think about statistical evidence and how you might know whether it's valid or reliable. *Validity*, by the way, refers to whether statistics accurately measure or reflect the subject they say they do. *Reliability* refers to whether they are consistent each time measurements or samples are taken. While no specific tests of credible statistics exist, three categories of questions can help guide your evaluation of statistical evidence:

1. **Objectivity**—Have these statistics been gathered for unbiased, scientific, or historical purposes? What's the reason the samples were taken in the first place? Does anyone hope to prove something by gathering and reporting this evidence, or is it objective in nature and purpose?

2. **Authenticity**—What do the figures really represent? Do they come from the source that reported them or did someone else gather them? Large drug companies often fund clinical trials of experimental pharmaceutical compounds because they hope to patent and sell the formulation once the Food and Drug Administration approves them. The results of the clinical trials may be accurate and unbiased, but knowing who paid for the experiments is helpful to the listener. Tobacco companies were notorious for producing scientific findings under the guise of "independent" research organizations that were actually established and funded by the cigarette industry.

3. **Carefulness of generalization**—What conclusions do the figures support? It's one thing to say that young women of childbearing age might benefit from taking 400 micrograms of folic acid each day, but it's unreasonable to generalize

health benefits to the population at large. Among the most frequent misuses of statistics is a simple tendency to over-generalize and say that the evidence means more or has wider application than the findings might warrant.

Carefully used and appropriately documented statistics, along with compelling testimony, provide your audience with good reasons to buy into your argument or point of view. To get them to trust you, though, you have to get them to trust your evidence. Reveal your sources, be specific, and stay within the bounds of reasonable generalization.

To get them to trust you, though, you have to get them to trust your evidence.

# TRUTH

22

## Structure can help carry an inexperienced speaker

Some years ago a college professor took a well-organized speech and scrambled it by randomly changing the order of its sentences. He then had a speaker deliver the original version to one group of listeners and the scrambled version to another group. After the speeches, he gave a test to see how well each group understood what they had heard. Not surprisingly, the group that heard the original, unscrambled presentation scored much higher than the other group.

A few years later, two professors repeated the same experiment at another school. But instead of testing how well the listeners understood each speech, they tested what effects the speeches had on the listeners' attitudes toward the speakers. They found that people who heard the well-organized speech believed the speaker was more competent and trustworthy than did those who heard the scrambled speech. These are just two of many studies that show the value of organization and structure in a presentation or speech. You undoubtedly know from personal experience that you appreciate and learn more from hearing a well-organized talk compared to one that's poorly organized or contains no internal structure.

Organization is important for two other reasons, as well. First, structure is closely connected to critical thinking. When you try to organize your presentation, you gain practice in the skill of establishing clear relationships among your ideas. Evidence also suggests that using a clear, specific method of organization can boost your confidence as a speaker and improve your ability to deliver a message fluently.

The second and equally important reason for organizing a presentation is that you'll save your audience the trouble of doing it for you. If you make them work at listening to and organizing your thoughts, evidence, and reasoning, they won't like it. Some, as you've seen, are highly motivated to learn what you're saying and will do the work

> When you try to organize your presentation, you gain practice in the skill of establishing clear relationships among your ideas.

necessary to make sense of it. Others won't even try and will just give up.

Presenters benefit from organizing a presentation, too. A message that unfolds as an orderly sequence of points is easier to remember and, therefore, takes less time to rehearse. As a result, the presentation itself is easy to give. Organization also helps minimize or eliminate rambling, which can undermine your effectiveness as a speaker and adversely affect the audience's perception of you as an expert worth listening to.

To help your audience understand your presentation, provide them with a quick look at it in a "blueprint" paragraph. This is a simple set of guideposts that follow your introduction and give the audience an opportunity to hear not only what you plan to talk about, but also the order in which you'll do it. Tell them what you plan to say and then keep your promise.

In addition to blueprinting your plan for the speech, you should reveal your main thesis or rhetorical purpose. Why are you speaking today? What's your intention for this presentation and this audience? What do you want of them?

Revealing your intentions is a good idea unless you believe or suspect that the audience disagrees with your viewpoint or conclusion. If you have the feeling they disagree with your thesis, start out slowly by focusing on issues and ideas you know they'll find agreeable and then move on to others that may be more problematic.

**This is a simple set of guideposts that follow your introduction and give the audience an opportunity to hear not only what you plan to talk about, but also the order in which you'll do it.**

Finally, you should make your pattern or structure clear to the audience, as well. If you've organized this presentation topic-ally, say, "I have just three main points and they are these . . . ." Or "I can think of four reasons why you should begin a program of systematic saving for retirement . . . ." If the pattern you've chosen has a chronological shape to it, tell them that. If you've selected a cause-and-effect order or a problem-solution order, explain that to your listeners. "I want to talk to you today about backdated stock options in our industry and explain to you, in detail, what this company has done to prevent abuses of the sort you've seen recently."

Some patterns of organization lend themselves more readily to some subjects than others. What matters most, though, is that you take the time and energy to impose some sort of structure on your presentation, and then explain it to your audience. You'll find it easier to give the speech if you do this, and  your audience will find it much easier to listen to your presentation.

# TRUTH

23

## Find support for your presentation

One of your most important tasks as a speaker is to select the type of evidence that is most likely to lead listeners to accept your point of view. So where do you find that material?

Broadly speaking, you have a choice between primary research and secondary research. Primary evidence is original or first-hand information that you gather yourself. Secondary evidence is all of the information gathered by other people. The main sources of primary research are interviews and surveys, while secondary research is available from literally millions of library and Internet resources. As you consider the wealth of evidence available to you, think about what your audience will find most interesting, convincing, and compelling. You're doing the research and gathering the evidence on their behalf.

The advantage of secondary research is, quite literally, that it's already been done for you. Professional librarians invest time and public resources thinking about what to archive, how to catalog it, and how to help you find it. A good librarian, in fact, is worth his weight in gold; all you have to do is explain, in general terms, what you're looking for and he will help you with the rest. Your public or university library's reference desk is a great place to start. Just present yourself as an interested, curious reader and the librarian will take it from there.

Among the assets you'll find in just about any library are bound volumes, periodicals, newspapers, and searchable databases. Libraries are famous for the vast number and quality of books they contain, but in many ways, these are among the least useful of the resources you'll find there. The real problem with books and bound volumes is that most of them are simply outdated. The process of writing, editing, and publishing a book is so time-consuming that by the time it reaches library or bookstore

**Think about what your audience will find most interesting, convincing, and compelling. You're doing the research and gathering the evidence on their behalf.**

shelves, the information is likely not as current as you may need. But the advantage of books is that they are carefully researched, professionally edited, and for the most part tend to focus on one coherent subject.

Newspapers and periodicals are not only more current, but they're also updated regularly. They frequently contain detailed evidence about current issues and events, as well as eyewitness testimony, expert opinion, and other information in the form of direct quotes. Newspapers are more up-to-date than magazines because they're published daily; their chief advantages are immediacy and detail. Magazines, on the other hand, devote most of their energy to summarizing what's happened in a particular field or area of interest over the past week or month. Some highly specialized periodicals are published quarterly and have a narrow but devoted following because of the intensity of their focus.

Increasingly, libraries are beginning to devote more time and money into searchable databases available on CD, DVD, and online. Most popular magazines are indexed in *Wilson Periodical Abstracts*, and most libraries offer access to the online databases InfoTrac Online, Expanded Academic ASAP, and EBSCO Academic Search Elite, all of which cover general periodicals and more specialized journals. For business-related topics, you may want to consider *ABI/Inform* and *Lexis-Nexis Academic University, Business*. The best way to find specific data, though, is to ask the librarian about the sort of information you're looking for, rather than specifying a particular database.

> Increasingly, libraries are beginning to devote more time and money into searchable databases available on CD, DVD, and online.

What if the library doesn't have the sort of information you're looking for? Let's say your task is to convince members of a neighborhood association that an amendment to the restrictive covenants on home remodeling is necessary. Books and periodicals won't help much with that subject. Although you may find that someone else has thought and written about this topic before, it's unlikely that those ideas will apply directly to the interests (and fears) of your neighbors. In this case, the subject is almost entirely local.

You might think about gathering primary evidence in the form of a survey. You could ask your neighbors about their own interests in remodeling or adding to their homes. You might get some sense of what interests them the most: a bigger garage, an additional bedroom, a screened back porch. Your survey data, even if it's not scientifically gathered as a stratified, random survey, might prove both useful and convincing to the directors of your neighborhood association. You can conduct this survey inexpensively on paper or online by using a survey service such as Zoomerang (http://info.zoomerang.com) or Survey Monkey (www.surveymonkey.com).

# 24

## Use the Internet to support your presentation

The Internet is a remarkably useful tool, both for business people and for others doing research or curious about subjects they'd like to know more about. Millions of computers linked together worldwide have instantaneous access to information about nearly any subject you can imagine.

The Internet, however, is not without its problems. For one thing, the information it contains is unorganized. I spoke with Stephen Hayes, a business-services librarian at the University of Notre Dame, who described the Internet as "a library with all the books on the floor." It's no ordinary library either. Literally anyone can set up a home page, buy a Web site address, and begin doing business on the Internet. So, a speechwriter in search of information can—and often does—find inaccurate information alongside valuable content on the Internet. "There's little we can do to verify the accuracy of the information contained in most sites on the World Wide Web," said Mr. Hayes. "Thus, each of us should approach what we find with appropriate caution and skepticism—just as we would a print source."

> A speechwriter in search of information can find inaccurate information alongside valuable content on the Internet.

The World Wide Web—the most heavily trafficked portion of the Internet—is organized broadly into four categories of sites: government, educational, commercial, and not-for-profit. Internet addresses, known as URLs (universal resource locators), reflect the specific category within the letters they contain. Corporate home pages (usually ending in ".com") will tell you things about a company that they want you to know, such as where to buy their products, how their stock price is doing, and how to apply for employment in the company. In many ways, these sites are simply another form of advertising.

Government-sponsored Web sites (ending in ".gov") provide large categories of information, including census data, international trade and banking data, and regulatory information. Educational institutions, such as colleges and universities, sponsor Web sites (ending in ".edu") that permit students, alumni, and others to find out more about everything from academic curricula to how the varsity lacrosse team is doing.

Finally, Web sites sponsored by not-for-profit organizations (usually ending in "org"), such as the American Red Cross, Goodwill Industries, and National Public Radio, offer everything from program schedules and broadcast transcripts to detailed descriptions of current activities in their organizations.

Search engines and directories are among the most useful tools to someone looking for information on the Internet. Simply speaking, search engines and directories are sophisticated programs that will look for information that you ask about. If you visit www.yahoo.com, you'll find one of the most popular and widely used directories. Simply type in the keywords that best describe the product, service, company, or industry that you want information about and the Yahoo! directory will produce numerous references with links to Web sites that may prove useful. *Directories* will search only the higher levels of a Web site, such as the title and author, while *search engines* will explore deeply into the data requested.

The more precisely or narrowly you define what you're looking for, the greater the chance that one of the more widely used search engines will find what you're seeking. Among the more popular search engines are www.hotbot.com, www.altavista.com, www.jeteye.com, and www.dogpile.com. The helpful site at www.searchengines.com provides tips and techniques for refining and improving your online searches. And, of course, the world's largest, most powerful, and most comprehensive search engine is www.google.com. At last count, Google had indexed nearly nine billion Web pages and provides a number of innovative and useful services, including GoogleScholar.com, which lets you search specifically for scholarly literature, including peer-reviewed papers, theses, books, preprints, abstracts, and technical reports from virtually all broad areas of research.

> The more precisely or narrowly you define what you're looking for, the greater the chance that one of the more widely used search engines will find what you're seeking.

Comparable new, specialized search engines are coming online all the time. The Web site 24HourScholar.com contains articles on subjects in the humanities, sciences, and social sciences. At FindArticles.com, you can cull articles from leading academic, industry, and general-interest publications. And www.answers.com is a reference search service that provides concise answers drawn from over a hundred authoritative encyclopedias, dictionaries, glossaries, and atlases.

The Internet is unbelievably useful for many reasons. It's ubiquitous; it's available 24 hours a day, 7 days a week; it's highly democratic in its approach to cataloging information; and, for the most part, it's free. Online sources also have a somewhat greater potential for up-to-date information. Books, journals, and other print materials take time to publish, but electronic documents can be posted to the Web as soon as they are created. Many organizations (including the U.S. government) now publish statistical information exclusively online.

The Internet also permits access to previously unavailable or hard-to-locate materials, including numerous collections posted by special-interest groups, nongovernmental agencies, and historical societies. Beyond that, online forums, including listservs, blogs, chat rooms, and discussion groups, can provide access to computer-mediated group discussions. Keep in mind two things about the quality of information available online. First, every entry is posted for a reason, and it's up to you to figure out the motives of the source. Second, not all Web entries are current, nor do they contain unbiased, entirely accurate information. It's also up to you to see if you can verify what you've found by comparing it with information available from reliable, well-known, credible sources.

> The Internet also permits access to previously unavailable or hard-to-locate materials, including numerous collections posted by special-interest groups, nongovernmental agencies, and historical societies.

# TRUTH
## 25

# Select a delivery approach

Most audience members are completely unaware of the delivery approach a presenter has selected...until they realize that someone is reading to them. For most audiences, that's a horrible feeling. Why? Because most people read aloud in a monotone voice, and unless they were trained as an actor or an announcer, most people can't handle a full script and an audience at the same time. The result: No eye contact, no vocal projection, and no sense of personal commitment to the presentation. The reaction: "Why am I here? He could have e-mailed this to me."

So, let's give some thought to methods of delivery. You have basically four options for delivering a presentation but probably shouldn't depend on more than just one or two of them.

*Memorized* presentations are delivered verbatim, word-for-word just as the authors wrote them. The problem with memorized speeches is that, unless you are a trained actor, you cannot deliver them with any level of conviction. They sound wooden, contrived, and artificial. Worse yet, you may forget where you are and have to start over. Unless you're doing Shakespeare from the stage, forget about memorized talks.

*Scripted* presentations are far more common among managerial and executive speaking events. The problem with speaking from a script, as I just noted, is that it sounds *read*. The impression from the audience is almost always negative. Reading a fully scripted speech ensures that you will include each key point and resist the temptation to ad-lib. But without a TelePrompter to display your script, you lose eye contact with the audience and seem distant or remote to them. You also drop your chin and compress the pitch of your voice. Unless you have no other choice, don't work with a verbatim script. If you must, then rehearse carefully and try looking up frequently, making regular eye contact with the audience.

> The problem with memorized speeches is that, unless you are a trained actor, you cannot deliver them with any level of conviction.

Even though I advise against reading from a script, keep in mind that it can serve a number of important functions for you and perhaps for your employer. First, it is one way of assuring that you'll deliver the speech exactly as written with no additions or deletions. Second, a script is a useful record of what you said to *this* audience on *this* occasion, just in case you're asked to speak to them again or, perhaps, asked to speak on the same topic to another group. Finally, a script is useful for security review. You can write the speech word-for-word, just as you plan to deliver it, and then show it to your supervisor or boss. If they think you're using this audience's time in an appropriate way and talking about information that's accurate, current, and suitable, they'll approve your remarks and you've bought yourself a small measure of support.

*Extemporaneous* presentations are, perhaps, your best alternative. These are speeches that are thoroughly researched, sensibly organized, well rehearsed, and delivered either without notes or with visual aids to prompt your memory. They are especially convincing to an audience because you make and maintain eye contact, you look at them rather than at a script, and you speak (seemingly) from the heart and not from a set of prepared notes. This is really the effect you are striving to achieve.

> Extemporaneous presentations...are speeches that are thoroughly researched, sensibly organized, well rehearsed, and delivered either without notes or with visual aids to prompt your memory.

*Impromptu* speeches are delivered without any preparation at all. Someone in charge usually asks you to stand up and "offer a few remarks." This is not the best approach to public speaking, obviously, since you have prepared nothing and haven't rehearsed. You may not even have a topic or an idea worth hearing. The good news is that the audience's expectations are low and they will applaud for nearly anything as long as it's brief and not insulting to them.

So what do you do when someone asks you to stand up and "offer a few remarks"? Modesty usually dictates that you say very little, but protocol usually demands that you say something. Here are a few ideas that may help:

- **Maintain your poise**—Just smile, thank your host for the opportunity to speak, and take advantage of the moment.

- **Decide on your topic and approach**—Speak briefly about something that you understand and that will be of interest to those listening. Select a pattern of organization and get going.

- **Do not apologize**—People know you didn't prepare a speech. Just talk to them.

- **Summarize your point and position**—In one sentence, or two at the most, underscore your key points and reiterate why they are important or worthwhile.

- **Be sincere, honest, and direct**—Nothing impresses an audience more profoundly than an honest person. Convey the impression that you have nothing to hide and nothing ulterior in your motives for speaking. They will reward you by considering your ideas and applauding your delivery.

The advice here is simple: Select an approach that best meets the needs and interests of the audience. People who speak from scripts (typically, executives who don't write their own speeches and frequently don't look at them until just before they're scheduled for delivery) are serving their own needs and not those of the audience. Your audience wants to hear from you, look you in the eyes, and get the sense that you're committed to the topic, the occasion...and to them. Your chances for success are directly related to some of the choices you make early in the process of putting your speech together.

# TRUTH

## 26

# Your introduction forms their first impression

How important is an introduction? Just ask Tufts University psychologist Nalini Ambady. She and a colleague videotaped 13 graduate teaching fellows as they taught their classes. She then took three random 10-second clips from each tape, combined them into one 30-second clip for each teacher, and showed the silent clips to students who did not know the teachers. The students rated the instructors on 13 variables, such as "accepting," "active," "competent," and "confident." Ambady combined these individual scores into one rating for each instructor and then correlated that rating with the teachers' end-of-semester evaluations from actual students.

"We were shocked at how high the correlation was," she said. "It was 0.76. In social psychology, anything above 0.6 is considered very strong." Curious to see how thin she could make the video slices before affecting the students' accuracy, Professor Ambady cut the length of the silent clips to 15 seconds, then to 6. Each time, the students accurately predicted the most successful teachers.

In his best-selling book, *Blink: The Power of Thinking Without Thinking*, author Malcom Gladwell explains at length how first impressions are not only lasting but frequently quite accurate. Although listeners sometimes make mistakes, particularly if they're focused on the wrong things at first, it's certainly true that they make judgments that are both durable and powerful in forming lasting impressions of the speaker and the subject.

Introductions serve a number of other functions in addition to creating an opportunity for listeners to form first impressions. At a primary level, a speech introduction arouses the audience's attention and provides them with an incentive

# First impressions are not only lasting but frequently quite accurate.

to listen. It also can provide some background on the speaker, the occasion, and the reasons for the speech itself. If someone else introduces you, of course, they'll do that for you. They'll also give the audience a chance to settle down; arrange their coats, briefcases, backpacks, and coffee cups; and perhaps turn off their cell phones. In the early moments of an introduction, few people are paying close attention to anything other than the fact that the presentation has begun. And that's fine because that's one of the purposes of an introduction.

The first few moments of a presentation also offer the opportunity for you to introduce your topic and the purpose of the speech—to preview your remarks and give the audience some sense of where this is headed. The blueprint, or overview of your main points, is customarily considered a part of the introduction, as well.

Among the more important components of an introduction is the *motivation step*. This is where you give the audience a reason (or reasons) to care about your subject and explain why you are there. A commonly effective approach to motivating an audience is to establish a link between the speaker and the values, needs, and interests of the audience. If the speaker can show that he has something important in common with members of the audience, perhaps they'll see the value in paying attention to and internalizing what the speaker has to say.

Nearly 50 years ago, American rhetorician Karl Wallace said that effective persuasion is about more than style and structure. It's about giving good reasons. This may sound as though Wallace had a firm grasp of the obvious, talking about giving proof for your arguments. He had more in mind, though. When he said "good reasons," he didn't mean reasons that *you* think are good. He meant reasons that the *audience* thinks are good. The motivations and reasoning of the audience are particularly powerful here. You can believe anything you want, no matter how irrational or nonsensical it may seem. But, if you want me (or others like me) to believe it, then you'll have to give reasons that *I* think are good. The introduction to your presentation is just the place to do that.

Finally, an introduction is precisely the right place for you to show your audience why the topic you chose is relevant to them and why you are qualified to talk about it. Showing the link to their lives, the relevance to decisions and choices they'll have to make, is crucial here. They all have a lot to think about in their day-to-day lives, and if you

**The motivation step is where you give the audience a reason (or reasons) to care about your subject and explain why you are there.**

can't show them that this subject is one more issue they should pay attention to, they'll simply tune out. The last link you have to make in your introduction is to yourself. If your host didn't introduce you to the audience, you'll have to do that for yourself and demonstrate why they should listen to you. Knowing your qualifications and experience—particularly with this topic—will help keep them with you long enough for you to offer up your evidence. That's asking a lot of an introduction, especially one that will take just a minute or less.

# TRUTH

27

## Begin with a purpose in mind

Give some thought to how you'll begin your talk, because your introduction is one of the most memorable aspects of the speech. The so-called primacy effect in psychology is a bias in the way people perceive and think about what they hear. Listeners are more likely to remember and believe what they hear first, rather than what they hear later on. This phenomenon is due to the fact that short-term memory at the beginning of a sequence of events is far less "crowded" and, because there are fewer items being processed in the brain, there is more time for rehearsal, consolidation, and storage of those events, which can later cause them to be transferred to long-term memory.

A good introduction takes advantage of the primacy effect by offering the most important and memorable aspects of the presentation in the first few minutes. The audience is eager to hear and think about your ideas. Don't disappoint them and don't waste time on issues that are

> Listeners are more likely to remember and believe what they hear first, rather than what they hear later on.

unrelated to your reasons for speaking. So, how should you begin? Many proven methods are available to you as you begin a speech. You might consider these:

**Begin with an anecdote**—Tell a story. People have loved listening to stories since they were kids, waiting for bedtime. Ronald Reagan's success as a speaker, in part, was due to his ability to "spin a yarn." Even those who disagreed with his politics acknowledged the importance storytelling played in his political life.

**Try humor**—People love to laugh, but be careful with this. Humor is great, unless you're not funny. Foremost among the occasions when you are likely not to be funny is when the joke is on the audience or someone they hold in high regard. Spontaneous, contemporary humor tends to work best. Stay away from set-piece jokes and amusing stories you recently heard.

**Offer a prediction**—Can you offer, based on the evidence you have gathered, a prediction that is likely to interest, amuse, frighten, or arouse your audience? Make sure you can support your contentions.

And make sure the evidence on which they are based is readily available and easily understood.

**Offer a dramatic forecast**—This is similar to a prediction, but longer-ranging in nature and usually involving extended or more complex events. David Walker, comptroller general of the United States, began a recent speech on the long-term fiscal health of the United States by forecasting a significant shift in the national debt because of entitlement programs. "I have some numbers for you this morning," he said. "They're all big, and they're all bad." He had our attention right away.

**Begin with a striking example**—This is just one form of an illustration or brief anecdote. If you can make your point by citing an example, do so. Just make sure you are not citing a notable exception to prove your point.

**Share a climactic moment**—Interesting speeches often base their central premise on an event or a particular moment in time. Audiences often find such examples powerful and easy to understand.

**Cite a suitable quotation**—You can find quotes everywhere. Rather than look in the usual sources (*Bartlett's Familiar Quotations, The Oxford Dictionary of Quotations*, or some similar volume), why not pick up the phone and talk with someone close to the subject? Get a reaction from a friend, family member, participant, or person who knows the events you are trying to describe. If that doesn't work, Bartlett's is now searchable online at www.bartleby.com. Just google the word "quotations" and you'll get more than thirty-five million hits. Surely you can find a quote in there somewhere.

> Interesting speeches often base their central premise on an event or a particular moment in time.

**Make a reference to the occasion**—A brief explanation about why you are glad to be there or why the occasion is special might generate interest in your talk while helping to humanize you to the audience.

**Ask a provocative question**—If you cannot predict the future with any measure of certainty, perhaps you can pose the issue in the form of a rhetorical question. "What would the world be like," said Dr. Paulette Gerkovich, "if there were no women in the workplace?" Her talk to college students on women in leadership positions began with a provocative examination of the roles they play in all segments of the workplace. She introduced her audience to an economy with half the workforce missing.

**Offer a statement of opinion**—This may work, although you should reveal the source of the opinion and the source should be both well known and respected by the audience. An opinion from someone they hold in low repute will do little to bolster your cause; it may actually damage your own credibility.

TRUTH

28

## Keep your audience interested

If you are worried about keeping your audience's attention as you speak, think about these ideas as you prepare your remarks:

**Provide order and structure—** If your audience is forced to work in order to follow your argument, they may lose interest. Make it easy for people to follow what you are saying: Provide an easy-to-understand structure that will carry your audience from one point to another.

> Provide an easy-to-understand structure that will carry your audience from one point to another.

**Keep it simple—**Your audience is going to come away with one or two of your main ideas. One or two. Not ten or fifteen. If you can't express in a sentence or two what you intend to get across, then your speech isn't focused well enough. If you don't have a clear idea of what you want to say, there is no way your audience will understand the key points.

**Keep it brief—**In New York a few years ago, a prominent steel company chief ended a 90-minute presentation before 400 of his executives and managers by striding from the stage and down the middle aisle. No one applauded until he was halfway out of the room. "They didn't know he was finished," a critic recalls. "They hadn't been attentive enough to recognize that."

**Talk, don't read—**Scripted speeches, particularly those written by someone other than the speaker, almost never sound authentic or convincing. I once asked a number of *Fortune 500* executives with samples of speeches they had given in the previous year. A friend who is a senior executive at PepsiCo said, "I hope you don't intend to use those speeches as teaching examples. Most chief executives," he said, "are terrible speakers simply because they won't give up the script." They bury their heads in the text, ignore the audience, and hope for the best. It rarely comes off the way they hope it will.

**Relax—**Breathing steadily and naturally will help you to focus; relax; and deliver a convincing, entertaining, and interesting speech. If you fall into a pattern of rapid, shallow breathing and can't seem to finish a sentence or a paragraph, just stop for a moment. Breathe deeply and then exhale. Bring your breathing under control once more and then continue.

**Use words they understand**—Plain English goes a long way toward winning friends and influencing people. The U.S. Securities and Exchange Commission has begun requiring the use of plain English in prospectuses, financial documents, and communication with investors. The idea is simple: If investors understand how their money is used, they'll make better investment decisions. The resulting markets are fairer and easier to understand for all who participate. Unless you are speaking with the hope that no one will understand you, plain English is the only sensible approach.

**Give them some information they can use**—Even the most charitable among your audience is likely to ask, "What's in this for me?" People may be polite enough to stay seated but may not pay close attention to your talk if their self-interests are not served. Give the audience something they can take to the bank, some ideas or information they can put to work as soon as they leave the room.

**Make your speech logical**—Not everyone is influenced by logic. Many people's minds, in fact, are easily swayed by an entirely illogical argument that contains just the right type and amount of emotion. For most of your audience, however, logic and rationality are important considerations. The more logical your arguments, the greater the chance your listeners will understand and adopt your viewpoint.

> Give the audience something they can take to the bank, some ideas or information they can put to work as soon as they leave the room.

**Make sure your viewpoint is reasonable**—A number of psychological studies show that adults will not engage routinely in behavior that they regard as unreasonable. Now, what's reasonable to one person may seem totally unreasonable to another, but the vast majority of people will remain consistent in their definitions of what is and is not reasonable. If you know your audience well, you have a better chance of convincing them to adopt your viewpoint, as long as what you ask of them falls within their established limits.

111

**Make sure your point is clear**—One reason many speeches fail is that the audience simply has no idea what the speaker wants. The main point is unclear, the supporting evidence is not well understood, or the conclusion is incomprehensible. Unless ambiguity is a deliberate part of your communication strategy, make sure your message, evidence, and intentions are clear to your listeners.

**Keep it moving**—Your audience will be patient with you for just so long. Don't try their patience and good nature by dragging the pace of your speech or dawdling on minor points. If your talk moves along briskly, chances are good that you'll maintain audience's interest.

**Answer their questions**—Every audience has questions. Your task is to solicit questions and answer them to their complete satisfaction. (See Truth 15, "Anticipate the questions your audience brings to your presentation.") If you are unwilling to address their questions, your audience is unlikely to pay attention or buy into your argument.

**Allay their fears**—Everyone in your audience is afraid of something. Find out what your audience fears. Some may worry that you will ask things of them that they are unwilling to do. Others fear that they won't understand the implications of your request. If you cannot dispel their fears, no audience will accept your point of view.

**Respect their needs**—Everyone in your audience has specific psychological needs. Each of them gathers and organizes information in slightly different ways. And each of them takes a slightly different approach to decision making. If you understand and respect their needs, they'll reward you. Some may have a need for details—show them the numbers. Others may have a need to understand where this idea fits in the larger scheme of things—show them the big picture. Still others may have a need to know who else has tried or approves of this idea—show them celebrity endorsements. If people have a specific need—say, a strong desire to know the source of your information—and you don't deal directly with that need, they're unlikely to adopt your viewpoint or do as you ask.

# 29

## Conclusions are as important as introductions

Conclusions are one of the most important (and most welcome) portions of any presentation. Why are they important? Well, for one thing, they offer one more opportunity to put your best evidence or most important ideas before your audience. They represent one last chance to say what you really mean, to reinforce your purpose for speaking, and to ask for their support or compliance. Conclusions also provide the audience with a sense of logical and emotional closure.

Like introductions, conclusions serve a number of purposes:

**Your conclusion signals the audience that the presentation is about to end**—A presentation is a journey of sorts for your audience, and you are their guide. It's important that you signal or cue them when you've come to the final portion of the talk. You might want to use a word or phrase that alerts them that you're about to finish: "finally," "in conclusion," "let me sum up by saying . . . ," "as I bring this to a close," or "let me close by saying . . . ."

That's also the appropriate moment to adjust your pacing, tone, pitch, and rhythm to indicate that this presentation is just about done. Don't fall prey to the temptation to keep speaking, though. Nothing is more annoying to the audience than a speaker who says, "In conclusion,"

> It's important that you signal or cue them when you've come to the final portion of the talk.

and then takes another 20 minutes to finish. An audience is forgiving of many things, but not of a speaker who overstays his welcome.

**Your conclusion helps summarize your main points**—As a U.S. Air Force officer, I had the opportunity to deliver a number of mission-related briefings to various people. Those presentations were intended to be cogent, informative, to the point, and useful to the audience. The advice from my commanders was always the same: "Tell them what you're going to tell 'em. Tell 'em. Then tell 'em what you just told 'em." Preview, main body, and conclusion in three short sentences. This is not bad advice, actually. Especially the part about "telling them what you told them." A solid summary provides your audience with a review of your main points (in order), their motivations for learning about and acting on them, and a final appeal that exhorts them to action.

**A good conclusion reiterates both the topic and purpose of the presentation**—Another important function of the conclusion is to restate the subject of your speech and the reasons for which you are speaking. Oklahoma University speech professor Dan O'Hair says, it's "to imprint it in the audience's memory."

**An effective conclusion challenges the audience to respond**—Depending on the speaker's intentions, the concluding remarks can include an appeal to the audience to respond in some way. Informative speeches usually include *descriptive* conclusions,

Restate the subject of your speech and the reasons for which you are speaking.

while *persuasive* speeches feature prescriptive conclusions. In describing what you want the audience to know or understand, the informative speaker usually summarizes the evidence, makes the key points clear, and re-motivates the audience to internalize the information just presented. A persuasive speaker, on the other hand, is an advocate on behalf of a particular point of view and, as such, is hoping for action on the part of the audience.

In a recent talk on the prospects for peace and stability in the Middle East, Shibley Telhami, a distinguished professor at the University of Maryland, concluded by saying, "I would suggest that our most important task in improving relations with Arab and Muslim countries and in spreading democracy is not through the rhetoric of reform and these high-powered moves that we make, but by putting far more resources into transforming the educational and economic possibilities for people in the Middle East. That could take us in the right direction." As a political scientist, he offered his audience a conclusion that included a call to action and suggested methods for reforming U.S. foreign policy. Although it did not ask specifically for action on the part of audience members, his intentions were clear, as was his request for all in the audience to see conflict in the Middle East in a new light.

Finally, you should give careful thought to making your conclusion memorable. How can you do this? You might think about the way you began: Use a quotation to stimulate audience thinking on this topic. You could pose a rhetorical question, asking what they hope for or what their plans are. You could conclude with a brief anecdote or humorous reference that captures the spirit of your speech. You might issue a challenge to those listening, or you could link back to the introduction and give the audience a sense of having come full circle. Above all else, leave them with a clear, simple, unambiguous message. Don't let them leave the room wondering what this speech was all about.

## Leave them with a clear, simple, unambiguous message.

# TRUTH

## 30

# Have confidence in your preparation

Everyone gets nervous before giving a presentation. Yes, even seasoned professionals with years of experience in public speaking say that they get just a bit nervous beforehand. But anxiety is a natural, normal response that you can learn to manage. I talk at greater length about managing anxiety and stage fright in Truths 32-35, but for now, focus on this principle: You'll perform better if you have confidence in your preparation.

If you thoroughly researched your topic, organized your material in a way that will make sense to the audience, and rehearsed your presentation carefully, you'll be fine. You simply need to trust the work you've done in preparation for the moment when you take the stage. You'll be nervous when you step up to the microphone, even the pros say that. But if you have confidence in the work you've done in advance of that moment, you'll do well.

A lesson from behavioral psychology might be helpful here. A scientific principle developed by Robert M. Yerkes and J. D. Dodson, known as the Yerkes-Dodson Law, demonstrates a clear relationship between arousal and performance. Their principle implies that, to a certain point, a certain amount of stress is healthy, useful, and even beneficial. This stress can inspire you to not only perform well in presenting, but also can improve your health and general well-being.

The stimulus of the human stress response is often essential for success. You see this commonly in situations such as sporting events, academic pursuits, and even in many creative and social activities. As stress levels increase, so does performance. This relationship between increased stress and increased performance does not continue indefinitely, however. Think of the relationship as a bell-shaped curve.

As stress increases, your performance increases until you reach the top of the curve. Then it

> Yerkes-Dodson Law demonstrates a clear relationship between arousal and performance. Their principle implies that, to a certain point, a certain amount of stress is healthy, useful, and even beneficial.

actually drops and continues dropping until it finally flattens out when it reaches conditions of intolerable stress. When stress exceeds your ability to cope, this overload contributes to diminished performance, inefficiency, and even adverse health problems. Ironically, as you move from the ten o'clock to the two o'clock position on the curve, your stress doubles but you gain nothing in productivity.

For peak performance, you want to stay near the top, just to the left side of the apex of the curve. Of course, this optimal level is not the same for everyone. An effective stress-management program can teach you where this optimal level of stress is for you personally, and it can help you reduce physical anxiety levels using both coping skills and relaxation techniques so that you stay out of the danger zone created by too much stress.

Getting too close to the top of the curve is not a good idea for ordinary, day-to-day activities for a couple of reasons. First, no one can run at maximum tempo all the time. Peak performance, day in and day out, exhausts even the fittest and most hardy person. Everyone needs to kick back and relax at regular intervals. Second, if you're constantly living at peak performance, you have no *surge capacity*, which is the ability to step up your performance output when you need it most.

So what are you to do when you walk up to the speaking platform, take the microphone, and greet your audience? Even experienced, professional speakers—actors, politicians, lecturers, professors— myself included, will tell you (if they're being honest) that they're always slightly nervous or a bit edgy. "I've never walked into a classroom," says a colleague at the University of Virginia's Darden School of Business, "without feeling somewhat anxious." How does he deal with that? "Well, there are a number of coping techniques," he replied, "but I just try to trust that the preparation I've done will carry me through."

He's absolutely right. Your preparations for a presentation were done under conditions of little or no stress, at a time when you were relaxed, confident, and under control. Just remember what you thought and how you felt when you completed your last rehearsal of the speech. Tell yourself that your research, organization, rehearsal, and visual aids will carry you through, and then trust in yourself as you step up to speak.

# TRUTH
# 31

## Repeat the process as often as possible

No one becomes a skilled or gifted public speaker by avoiding the experience. The best speakers and presenters, in fact, are those who do it frequently and who enjoy the experience. Public speaking is never pleasant at first, of course, because you're still struggling with the basics of organization, evidence, and delivery—not to mention adjusting to the audience, the occasion, and the experience of being in front of all those people.

The truth about presenting, however, is that you'll get much better at it if you do it frequently. So the advice here is simple: Repeat the process as often as possible. Seek out opportunities to speak to your colleagues, friends, coworkers, clients, customers, and others. Don't turn down an opportunity to give a presentation if your boss or friends should ask you to do just that.

Perhaps another lesson from behavioral psychology will reinforce this concept: Behavior is affected by its consequences. You reward and punish people, for example, so that they will behave in ways that you consider desirable or appropriate. Edward L. Thorndike studied the effects of this consequence in a well-known experiment. He enclosed a cat in a box, but provided the possibility for escape if the cat could figure out how the latch mechanism worked. The cat eventually moved the latch,

## Behavior is affected by its consequences.

which opened the door. When repeatedly enclosed in a box, the cat gradually stopped doing those things that were proven ineffective and made the successful response very quickly.

Subsequent experiments by B.F. Skinner and others have shown that an animal's repeated success results in reinforcement of useful or desired behaviors, while unsuccessful (or painful) experiences result in the extinction of behaviors that are neither useful nor productive. In essence, productive behaviors are reinforced, while negative or inconsequential behaviors are abandoned.

What do cats trying to escape from a box have to do with presenting? Well, humans react in much the same way as cats when confronted with stressful situations, and both will exhibit behaviors that are proven most useful or productive. In the case of the human presenter, the audience reinforces those behaviors that they find most relevant and productive. If the speaker offers a pattern of organization that makes sense, or evidence that seems convincing, they reward the speaker with their attention, eye contact, engaged posture, and more. If the presentation goes especially well, the audience reinforces the experience with their sustained, appreciative applause. Many individuals from the audience may approach the speaker afterward, offering congratulations and thanks, and asking additional questions about the subject. It's a very positive and rewarding experience for the speaker.

The opposite can be true, as well. If the speaker doesn't offer up anything relevant or useful for the audience, or if they feel the speaker is wandering or dragging out the experience, some in the audience will yawn, look at their watches (or worse, their cell phones), and appear bored and disengaged. If it really gets bad and the audience thinks the presentation is a total waste of time, some may get up and leave. At the extreme, some audience members may begin heckling or talking back to the speaker, creating a strongly negative experience for him. That's

> If the presentation goes especially well, the audience reinforces the experience with their sustained, appreciative applause....It's a very positive and rewarding experience for the speaker.

the point when it's useful to know which behaviors on the speaker's part have produced the negative response from the audience.

Speaking frequently, however, will lead you to become a more sincere, confident, well-adjusted presenter. You cannot determine which patterns of organization, turns of phrase, or forms of expression will work best with an audience unless you try them out. You cannot become a better speaker by just listening to and watching others. That's helpful, of course. I've asked you to emulate speakers whom you admire and think are good. But eventually, you have to get up and do it for yourself. And you have to repeat the experience as often as possible. The more you speak, the better you'll perform on each occasion.

# TRUTH

## 32

# All speakers get nervous

When people stand up to speak in front of others, they are inevitably nervous. Some just a little; others a lot. Even skilled professionals who conduct dozens of presentations a year will admit to being at least a little anxious before a speech. Nervousness is a perfectly normal reaction to a stressful situation.

So, why do people see a presentation as stressful? What's stressful about talking to a few people about a subject you know and like? First, it may not be just a few people. The audience may be large and include people you don't know well. Second, the subject may not be one you know *or* like. You may speak on a topic that was assigned to you by a supervisor and address a group of people you've just met.

People generally get anxious about public speaking situations for three reasons:

> The best defense, of course, is careful, thorough preparation.

1.  **Fear of being unprepared**—This fear is actually rational. If you're unprepared, you really should feel afraid. The source of the anxiety is the idea that you'll forget what you planned to say, you won't think of examples that the audience will find convincing, and you'll present your key points out of order. The best defense against this, of course, is careful, thorough preparation. Do your research, think extensively about your pattern of organization, look for motivation and proof the audience will find compelling, and practice what you plan to say.

2.  **Fear of being evaluated**—No one likes being judged by others. It's a potentially humbling, embarrassing experience. The fact is, though, that the audience will take their measure of you and form a judgment regarding your expertise, competence, and relevance. Take that as a challenge and prepare for it. What matters most to them is what you can do for them, so make absolutely certain you have ideas and concepts they can use. Focus on issues that are of greatest concern to them; deal with their fears and provide them with information that will make their lives easier, better, safer, and more meaningful. When they compare the experience of listening to you with how they might have spent the time somewhere else, you'll get a favorable judgment.

3. **Fear of the unknown**—U.S. Air Force test pilot Chuck Yeager was once asked by a cadet whether he was afraid of anything the day he became the first to fly faster than the speed of sound. "Afraid of anything?" he replied. "What do you have in mind?" The cadet thought for a moment and said, "Well, afraid of the unknown." The general paused momentarily and then said, "I take known risks, risks I know I can manage. It's just not productive for me to worry about the unknown."

General Yeager made a good point. Work on those things that you know are important to the audience. Don't worry about issues you can't control. Focus on the expectations of the audience and the promise you made when you agreed to give the presentation. Worrying about whether the slide projector will work or whether the audience will like the way you're dressed is pointless. Do your best to control those things you can influence and simply let go of the rest.

> Work on those things that you know are important to the audience. Don't worry about issues you can't control.

Recognize that feeling anxious before a speech is a natural response to a potentially stressful situation, then do what you can to make it less stressful by preparing thoroughly, focusing on the audience, and doing what you *can* to put yourself in a positive state of mind.

# TRUTH

## 33

# Recognize anxiety before it begins

The best way to deal with anxiety in a presentation is to recognize it before it begins. The audience won't know you're nervous unless you tell them you are (my advice: don't) or they see and hear nervousness once you begin speaking. If you deal with your nerves in advance, then your chances for a successful presentation are much greater.

Behavioral psychologists commonly recommend three ways to diminish the negative effects of anxiety. These include depersonalization, behavior modification, and practice:

1.  **Depersonalization**—This technique requires that you think of your speech in terms that aren't personal to you. Some degree of anxiety flows out of personal concerns: "Will the audience understand my argument?" "What if I offend somebody?" "Do I look all right?" These are natural concerns, but they can debilitate a speaker who focuses on herself rather than the content of the speech. The audience is much more interested in the subject of your talk than they are in you as a person. Once you become a celebrity, of course, that may change; but for now, they're focused on content. So should you.

2.  **Behavior modification**—Trying to completely relax during a speech is both understandable and impossible. Audiences expect a speaker to be intense about the subject matter, but intensity is not the same thing as anxiety, and you should focus all of your energy on suppressing your nerves.

    Some of the more common symptoms of a nervous speaker are trembling, fidgeting, a weak or quivering voice, and losing your concentration—all of which are correctable. These symptoms are usually most acute at the beginning of a speech and generally dissipate as a speaker moves into the heart of the argument. In fact, by the end of most speeches, there are usually no outward signs of anxiety for even the most nervous speakers.

    So, if you're feeling anxious as a presentation begins, make certain that you've done all you can in advance to make this a comfortable moment. Your first priority is to breathe properly. Nervousness can cause you to take shallow, quick breaths that often translate into a reedy, panicked voice. Before you step up to the podium, consciously take a couple of long, deep breaths. Not only will such breathing patterns contribute to a stronger voice, but they will also help you to relax.

Second, the opening of your presentation should be very familiar to you. This is an especially important, memorable part of your talk, so you should over-rehearse it. That's right, *over*-rehearse. Practice it again and again, until it flows easily and comes naturally to you.

> Before you step up to the podium, consciously take a couple of long, deep breaths. Not only will such breathing patterns contribute to a stronger voice, but they will also help you to relax.

3. **Practice**—I've already mentioned the value of rehearsal, but it's worth repeating. A huge measure of your confidence as a speaker comes directly from the knowledge that you've worked on a talk at great length. This means not merely reading your script or notes from a laptop screen. You should stand up, speak aloud, and time yourself as you move along. You should do all that you can to create the same conditions you'll face as a presenter and make certain you know what's coming next. Depending on the complexity or newness of your speech content, you may want to rehearse three or four times before giving your presentation to an audience for the first time.

# TRUTH

## 34

## Deal with nervous behaviors

The best way to deal with nervous behaviors is to take an inventory of them during practice sessions. Unfortunately, most nervous behaviors are neither obvious nor self-evident. Watching a videotape of yourself as you speak or asking a friend or colleague to critique you are two helpful ways to discover what you look and sound like when you speak. If your behavior betrays a bad case of nerves, you'll know what to look for and how to control it.

What are the most common behaviors to look for in a nervous speaker? These four are most prevalent:

> Watching a videotape of yourself as you speak or asking a friend or colleague to critique you are two helpful ways to discover what you look and sound like when you speak.

1.  **Fidgeting with something as you speak**—Don't bring a pen, paper clip, or rubber band with you to the podium. These things inevitably end up in your hands and you will likely end up playing with them unconsciously. Once that begins, the audience will see or think of little else. You should also avoid touching your hair and playing with keys or coins in your pockets. Try to avoid scratching yourself (anywhere) because it really bothers the audience. The same applies to clasping your hands behind your back, swaying back and forth, and nervous foot movement.

2.  **Trembling**—Trembling hands are a common symptom of nervousness. The best place for your hands is generally at your side, but grasping the podium lightly is a good way to respond to trembling. Holding note cards or papers only magnifies trembling hands, so put them down and either work without them or glance at them only occasionally. Simple, controlled gestures helps, too. By gesturing, you dispel nervous energy, engage the audience, and help to relax your upper body muscles.

3.  **Quivering voice**—A strong voice is essential in conveying commitment and sincerity to your audience, and anxiety can weaken your voice to an extent. There are ways to address

this issue, but you must try not to create other problems as you attempt to solve this one. Speaking a bit more loudly and deeply is a useful technique to soften a quivering voice, as long as you don't speak too loudly or too deeply. If your voice is too loud, you'll have little opportunity to adjust volume as you move through the speech, and if your voice is too deep, you'll just sound silly.

4. **Forgetting what you want to say**—This symptom can be horrific, but only if you let it disrupt the flow of your presentation. Some speakers try to overcome this problem by writing out their speeches, word-for-word. That doesn't often work very well, though, because reading from a script takes your eyes off the audience and drops your head and chin, which compresses your vocal cords. And unless you're a trained announcer or actor, you're likely to sound unnatural as you read from a script. A better strategy is to rely on brief, compact notes that will help refresh your memory as you move from point to point. If you really do forget what you want to say, then you can take a sip of water and take a moment to regain your composure. The audience will readily forgive you for opening your water bottle and taking a drink, as long as you don't do it often. Openly admitting that you've lost your train of thought and then re-focusing on the main point may work as well, but it's a trick you can use just once during a speech.

> Openly admitting that you've lost your train of thought and then re-focusing on the main point may work as well, but it's a trick you can use just once during a speech.

Once you identify the outward symptoms of nervousness, you can work during rehearsals to minimize or eliminate them. Becoming aware of how you look and sound as you speak is the first step in becoming a more confident, sincere presenter.

# 35

## Keep your nervousness to yourself

Despite your best efforts to depersonalize, to modify your behavior, and to practice in advance of a presentation, you may still find that you're a bit nervous just before you begin. Here's a time-honored truth about that moment: Keep your nervousness to yourself.

No one in the audience cares or is interested in the fact that you're nervous. They have issues of their own to worry about. They expect, in fact, that you'll be interesting, relevant, witty, and helpful. They may (or may not) have had a choice about attending your presentation. If they did so voluntarily, they've clearly voted in favor of listening to you, and you should see that as a positive thing. Even if they're non-volunteers, they're still holding out hope that this talk may, somehow, prove interesting or useful.

Sharing the depth or intensity of your anxiety with them will not help things a bit. The audience just doesn't want to hear about it. The more humane and empathetic among them will hope for the best, silently cheering for you to overcome your fears and deliver a brilliant speech, but they certainly don't want you to remind them of how difficult this is for you.

Keep in mind that your mood—that is, your emotional state—is both transparent and infectious. People in the audience will know in fairly short order just how you feel about them, your topic, and the occasion. If you feel enthusiastic about being there, they'll sense that. If you're uncertain or unsure of yourself, they'll know. And, if you're hyperventilating and panicky, they'll pick up on that. You can't really hide your feelings from the audience. Even small children are adept at sensing how other humans feel. The cues are almost entirely nonverbal: Your posture, gestures, facial expression, breathing rate, eye contact, pacing, phrasing, vocal control, and more will reveal to the audience how you feel about being there at that moment. That's what I mean by transparent.

> Your mood—that is, your emotional state—is both transparent and infectious.

By infectious, I mean that the audience (or some of them, at least) are likely to begin feeling just as you do. Are you antsy or unhappy with the experience of standing there? Well, so are they. Do you feel like this isn't going well? They may share that thought. Do you want this to be over? They probably do, as well.

Although you can't fool them about how you feel, it is actually possible to convince yourself that you're doing better than you thought you might. First, concentrate on what's going right. Did you arrive on time? Have you found the right auditorium? Is the projection equipment working? Have you taken a moment to greet your host or meet the person who will introduce you? Focus on those elements of the presentation that have gone exactly as planned, and you'll begin to feel better.

Second, concentrate on your preparation. Take another look at your notes and recall to yourself how thoroughly you researched the subject, how carefully you organized the evidence, and how well you've taken the needs of the audience into consideration. Then think back on the number of times you rehearsed the presentation. All of

> Focus on those elements of the presentation that have gone exactly as planned, and you'll begin to feel better.

this helps you to calm down, breathe easily, and focus on the value of what's about to happen. Think positively and you are much more likely to deliver a relaxed, professional, and sincere presentation.

# TRUTH

## 36

## Most information is transferred nonverbally

Communication experts have established the fact that less than a third of the meaning transferred from one person to another in a personal conversation comes from the words that are spoken. The majority of meaning comes from nonverbal sources, including body movement, eye contact, gestures, posture vocal tone, pitch, pacing, and phrasing. Other messages come from your clothing, your use of time, and literally dozens of other nonverbal categories. People learn how to read and interpret such wordless messages, but many of these messages are difficult to detect and understand.

Nonverbal communication is widely regarded as the transfer of meaning without the use of verbal symbols. That is, *nonverbal* refers in a literal sense to those actions, objects, and contexts that either communicate directly or facilitate communication without using words. But as communication professionals and casual observers alike will testify, separating the effects of verbal and nonverbal behavior is never easy, largely because they tend to reinforce each other, contradict each other, or are in some way *about* each other.

Virtually all nonverbal communication is culturally based, with the exception of emotional displays and certain facial expressions. That is, you learn to behave and communicate in certain ways, and to interpret the meanings of those behaviors, as you grow up in your culture. This means acquiring values, beliefs, possessions, behaviors, and ways of thinking that are acceptable to others and, in fact, expected of you as a member of your society. So, what is strictly forbidden in one culture—exposing an adult woman's face to strangers in public—is perfectly normal in another. As a member of a global community, you must not only learn and abide by the rules of the society you grew up in, but also come to understand and appreciate the rules of other societies, as well.

> Separating the effects of verbal and nonverbal behavior is never easy, largely because they tend to reinforce each other, contradict each other, or are in some way *about* each other.

What does this mean for you as a speaker? It means several things. First, it means that your audience has certain expectations of you. They pay attention, for example, to how you're dressed. With very few exceptions, the rule is simple: You

## You should dress just slightly better than others in the room.

should dress just slightly better than others in the room. Appropriate attire creates the impression that you are organized, professional, and on top of your game. It also conveys the notion that you respect your audience and want to create a positive image in their minds.

Audience expectations are an important consideration. Any customer service manager will tell you that a sales professional's job is to meet or exceed the customer's expectations. The same is true of a public speaker. Following a presentation to mid-level managers of Bayer Corporation (whose parent company is the German chemical and pharmaceutical firm, Bayer AG), I was approached by Helge Weymeyer, CEO of the company. He thanked me for my talk to his managers and then asked me about a couple of nonverbal issues that interested him. "Why have you removed your suit jacket?" he enquired. "Well, to put the audience at ease," I said. "Yes," he replied, "but I am already at ease. It's unprofessional to speak without a jacket." He wasn't done with me. "I want to know why you stand in the center of the room, walk about, and approach people as you speak." I thought about that for a moment and asked him, "Where do you think I should be?" "Where you belong," he said, "behind the podium, reading from your script."

The expectations of a German audience are not necessarily the same as those of a North American audience, and I failed to consider what they might be looking for in a speaker. Granted, we were on my turf, but their expectations were still somewhat different. Think carefully about how each element of your nonverbal presence in the room affects the audience: your appearance, movement, eye contact, vocal tone, pacing, pitch, and phrasing. Do all that you can to create a positive, interesting experience for those in your audience.

# 37

# The nonverbal process can work for you

Audience members pay attention to a number of things as they listen to a presentation, including the words the speaker is saying, the rate at which they're spoken, the emphasis given to certain words, the depth and strength of the speaker's voice, the confidence and sincerity the speaker conveys, and much more.

The audience also pays attention to the context in which the presentation takes place. How are the seats arranged? Are they comfortable? Is the room warm or cool enough? Can all members of the audience see the speaker adequately? Can they hear the speaker? Many of them aren't paying attention to *verbal* issues—that is, the words that the speaker says. Much of what they are focusing on has little to do with the verbal message. These nonverbal cues are important to the audience, though, or they wouldn't pay attention to them.

How does the process of communicating nonverbally work? You can't go to a dictionary to look up a gesture or a facial expression. Human movement, eye contact, and vocal tone don't always have a direct verbal translation. So what's going on here? Nonverbal communication is a three-step process involving a cue, your own expectations, and an inference.

1.  **Cue**—You look first for a wordless cue—a motion, perhaps, or an object. For example, on arriving at work in the morning, you notice a co-worker who is glum, sullen, and withdrawn. You say "Good morning," but he doesn't reply. Your cues are nonverbal: his facial expression, body posture, and failure to respond to your greeting.

2.  **Expectation**—You then match the cues against your expectations, asking what seems reasonable or what seems obvious, based on your prior experiences. Because your co-worker is normally cheerful, talkative, and outgoing, your expectations conflict with the cues you just picked up. Your expectations are important, because you won't know what to make of a cue if you have no prior experience with it. For example, when you

You won't know what to make of a cue if you have no prior experience with it.

meet someone new or when you travel to a foreign country for the first time, you're not entirely sure what to expect.

3.  **Inference**—After picking up a cue and measuring its importance and meaning against your expectations, you then *infer* meaning. Since you can't see an attitude or intention directly, you must draw an inference based on the nonverbal cue and your own expectations. Given the cue and your expectations of your co-worker in this example, you conclude that he's unhappy, upset, or depressed for some reason. Note that this conclusion is based on observation alone and not an exchange of verbal information between two people. If you are perceptive and observant, you can learn a great deal without the use of language. But use caution when interpreting nonverbal cues. Often your confidence will exceed your ability to interpret cues accurately.

> You must draw an inference based on the nonverbal cue and your own expectations.

Keep in mind that the United States is a *low-context* society. This means that somewhat less communication takes place as a result of context, such as time of day, location, who's in the room, whether you've met these people before, and so on. More meaning is transferred in the U.S. as a direct result of what people say to one another. In a *high-context* society, such as Japan, China, Mexico, Saudi Arabia, or the Philippines, the context of the communication is much more important. People in those societies pay closer attention to whether this is your first trip there or your fifth, whether they're meeting with the chief executive or a mid-level manager, and much more. In those cultures, and in dealing with people from those societies, attention to nonverbal issues as you speak (and as you listen) becomes increasingly important.

# TRUTH

## 38

# Nonverbal communication has specific functions

If an important fraction of the information transferred from speaker to listener comes in the form of something other than words, then you should understand the roles that such communication can play in the exchange. Nonverbal communication serves a number of important functions for public speakers, but researchers have identified these six as major functions:

1. **Accenting**—Nonverbal communication often highlights or emphasizes some part of a verbal message. A raised eyebrow might accompany an expression of surprise; a wagging finger might underscore an expression of disapproval.

2. **Complementing**—Nonverbal communication also reinforces the general tone or attitude of your verbal communication. A downcast expression and slumping posture might accompany words of discouragement or depression; upright posture, a smile, and animated movement might reinforce a verbal story about winning a recent promotion.

3. **Contradicting**—On the other hand, nonverbal communication can also contradict the verbal messages you send, sometimes deliberately or sometimes unintentionally. Tears in your eyes and a quiver in your voice might involuntarily contradict a verbal message telling friends and family that you're doing all right. A wink and a nod might deliberately send the nonverbal message that what you're saying just isn't so. The truth is, when verbal and nonverbal messages contradict each other, people tend to believe the nonverbal.

> When verbal and nonverbal messages contradict each other, people tend to believe the nonverbal.

In the final analysis, it's simply much easier to lie than it is to control a range of nonverbal reactions, such as facial expression, pupil dilation, tension in your vocal cords, pulse rate, sweating, muscle tone, and so on. Control of such things is, for most people, well beyond their voluntary reach.

**4.** **Regulating**—Certain nonverbal movements and gestures are used to regulate the flow, pace, and back-and-forth nature of verbal communication. When you want someone to speak to you, you face that person, open your eyes, open your arms with hands extended and palms facing upward, and look expectantly into his eyes. When you want to stop someone from speaking so you can either talk or think of what you're about to say, then you will turn slightly away, fold your arms, put one hand out with palm facing forward, and either close your eyes or turn your head away.

**5.** **Repeating**—Nonverbal messages can also repeat what verbal messages convey. With car keys in hand, and coat and hat on, I can announce, "I'm leaving now," as you walk toward the door. You might hold up three fingers as you ask, "Remember to pick up ice at the grocery store. We're going to need three bags for tonight's reception."

**6.** **Substituting**—Nonverbal communication can also substitute for, or take the place of, verbal messages, particularly if they're simple or brief. As a youngster looks toward a parent on the sidelines during an athletic contest, a quick "thumbs up" can substitute for words of praise or encouragement that might not be heard from a distance or in a noisy crowd.

> Nonverbal communication can also substitute for, or take the place of, verbal messages.

Understanding the functions of nonverbal mannerisms and how they're likely interpreted can help you as a speaker, especially if the topic or you are new to an audience.

# 39

# Nonverbal communication is governed by key principles

After 75 years of social science research and 5,000 years of human experience, six principles of nonverbal communication are considered universally true:

1.  **Nonverbal communication occurs in a context**—Just as context is important to the meaning of verbal messages, so is context important to your understanding of nonverbal messages. Folded arms and laid-back posture may mean disinterest or boredom on one occasion but may signify introspective thought on another. Professor Joseph DeVito of Hunter College says, in fact, that "Divorced from the context, it is impossible to tell what any given bit of nonverbal behavior may mean.... In attempting to understand and analyze nonverbal communication...it is essential that full recognition be taken of the context."

2.  **Nonverbal behaviors are usually packaged**—Nonverbal behavior, according to most researchers, occurs in *packages* or *clusters* in which the various verbal and nonverbal messages occur more or less simultaneously. Body posture, eye contact, arm and leg movement, facial expression, vocal tone, pacing and phrasing of vocal expressions, muscle tone, and numerous other elements of nonverbal communication all happen at once. Isolating one element of the cluster from another without taking all of them into account is difficult.

3.  **Nonverbal behavior always communicates**—All behavior communicates, so you are always communicating, even when you aren't speaking with or listening to others. Even the least significant of your behaviors, such as your posture, the position of your mouth, or the way you tuck (or fail to tuck) in your shirt, say something about your professionalism to others around you. Other people may not interpret those behaviors in the same way or in the way you might want them to, but like it or not, you're always communicating, even if you're just sitting there

> You are always communicating, even when you aren't speaking with or listening to others.

"doing nothing." Doing nothing, in fact, may communicate volumes about your attitude.

4.  **Nonverbal behavior is governed by rules**—Linguistics is devoted to studying and explaining the rules of language. And just as spoken and written languages follow specific rules so does nonverbal communication. A few forms of nonverbal behavior, such as facial expressions conveying sadness, joy, contentment, astonishment, or grief, are universal. That is, the expressions are basically the same for all humankind, regardless of where you are born, raised, or educated. Most of your nonverbal behavior, however, is learned and is a product of the culture in which you are raised. A motion or hand gesture may well mean something entirely different in another culture. Touching the thumb and forefinger together to form a circle typically signifies everything is "A-OK" in North America. But in Latin America, that same gesture is a powerful insult.

> A motion or hand gesture may well mean something entirely different in another culture.

5.  **Nonverbal behavior is highly believable**—Researchers have discovered what we have known individually for quite some time: People are quick to believe nonverbal behaviors, even when they contradict verbal messages. When an employee's eyes dart away quickly or search the floor as she thinks of an answer to a supervisor's question, most people would suspect the employee is not telling the truth. Try as you might, you cannot fake many nonverbal behaviors. You might convincingly write or speak words that are untrue, but behaving nonverbally in ways that are false or deceptive is more difficult.

6.  **Nonverbal behavior is meta-communicational**—The word *meta* is borrowed from Greek and means "along with, about, or among." Thus *meta-communication* is communication *about* communication. The behaviors you exhibit while communicating are actually about communication itself, and nonverbal communication occurs in reference to the process of communicating. Your facial expression reveals

how you feel about the meal you are served; your handshake, vocal tone, and eye contact tell what you think about the person you've just met.

40

# Nonverbal communication has an effect on your audience

Here are six general outcomes of nonverbal communication that are important for every presenter to know:

1. **Nonverbal cues are often difficult to read**—Some years ago, a number of popular books introduced the general public to nonverbal communication. One popular volume, *Body Language*, described the nonverbal studies of several researchers. This best-seller was followed by other books that simplified and popularized research in this area. Many of them, however, oversimplified the behavioral science behind the findings in the interest of making a sale, detecting a liar, attracting members of the opposite sex, and so on.

   According to Professor Mark Knapp of the University of Texas, "Although such books aroused the public's interest in nonverbal communication...readers too often were left with the idea that reading nonverbal cues is *the* key to success in any human encounter; some of these books implied that single cues represent single meanings. Not only is it important to look at nonverbal *clusters* of behavior, but also to recognize that nonverbal meaning, like verbal, rarely is limited to a single denotative meaning."

2. **Nonverbal cues are often difficult to interpret**—What may mean one thing in one context, culture, or circumstance may mean something entirely different in another. Professor Knapp goes on to say, "Some of these popularized accounts do not sufficiently remind us that the meaning of a particular behavior is often understood by looking at the context in which the behavior occurs; for example, looking into someone's eyes may reflect affection in one situation and aggression in another." The importance of reading context, just as you would with verbal expression, is especially important. The meaning of all communication, after all, is context-driven.

   > The meaning of all communication, after all, is context-driven.

3. **Nonverbal behaviors are often contradictory**—Your posture and vocal tone may say one thing, but your eyes may say another. You try to stand up straight and portray a dominant, confident posture, but your hands are fidgeting with a pen, which may say something entirely different. Nonverbal behaviors do come "packaged" together, and you must often examine several behaviors before you begin to discern a coherent picture of the person in front of you.

4. **Some nonverbal cues are more important than others**— As you examine several behaviors clustered together—vocal pace, tone, and pitch; body posture; pupil dilation; arm and hand movements—careful observers clearly see that some cues are more important than others. The relative importance of a given cue is dependent on the habits and usual behaviors of the speaker. In other words, are the behaviors you're observing usual or unusual for this person? If they're unusual, do they contradict verbal portions of the message? And, finally, you should note that some portions of your anatomy are simply easier to control than others: Even a nervous person can sit still if he makes a determined effort to do so, but few among us can control the pupils' dilation. Many can control facial expression, but few can determine when tears will flow or when their voices will choke with emotion.

5. **You often read into some cues much that isn't there, and fail to read some cues that are clearly present**—You often look for cues that seem most important to you personally: whether a person looks you directly in the eyes as you speak or which direction you cross your legs. Such cues may be meaningless. You can also misread cues if you have insufficient information on which to base a judgment. Business leaders seen nodding off in a conference are judged as indifferent by their hosts; in reality, jet lag may have caught up with them.

6. **You're not as skilled at this as you think you are; your confidence often exceeds your ability**—Be cautious. Even though a substantial portion of what you learn from human interaction—between two-thirds and three-quarters of all meaning—comes from nonverbal cues, you simply aren't as skilled at this as you'd like to be. You can easily misinterpret,

misread, or misunderstand someone. And you can just as easily jump to conclusions from only a few bits of evidence. The best advice is to withhold judgment as long as possible, gather as much information—verbal as well as nonverbal—as possible, and then reconfirm what you think you know as frequently as possible.

# TRUTH

41

## Visual aids can help your audience understand your message

Behavioral scientists know that visual images can have a powerful effect on the process of learning. In some instances, the use of pictures may reach people who simply don't listen well to the spoken word or who may not understand what the words mean.

Professor G. M. Ingersoll discovered in his studies at Penn State University that some people pay more attention to what they see than what they hear. That means, of course, that some people remember more of what they see, while others remember more of what they hear. The reasons for this phenomenon are complex and may have more to do with the way people's brains are organized than their preferences for pictures or sound. In his experiments, Professor Ingersoll found that some people more quickly and readily recall information and concepts that have a visual component. Others are more in tune to the spoken word.

The implication for public speakers seems clear: While visual information may explain or reinforce spoken information, it may also reach a significant number of audience members who do not readily attend to, understand, or remember the spoken word. Other behavioral scientists have found that a word plus a related picture combination is superior to either words or pictures alone when testing an audience to recognize an idea or concept.

**Some people remember more of what they see, while others remember more of what they hear.**

So, what does this mean for you? Several things. First, research clearly shows that visual support helps to explain, reinforce, and clarify the spoken word during a presentation. That means if you can't *say* it easily, you can *show* it to your audience. The research clearly implies something important for all speakers. If some people pay more attention to what they see and others to what they hear, then don't leave anyone out. Say it to them, show it to them, and tell them where they can find more information.

Visual information tends to work best when you have new data for your audience or when the information you hope to convey is complex or technical in nature. Visuals are also helpful if your message is coming to them in a new context. Numbers, quick facts, quotes, and lists frequently benefit from some form of visual display. And, unquestionably, showing your audience comparisons in visual form is easier than telling them and helps them to understand how one item compares to another over time

**Say it to them, show it to them, and tell them where they can find more information.**

or in cumulative effect. Finally, geographical or spatial patterns are often easily conveyed in visual displays.

Good visuals also have a number of characteristics in common. First, they're almost always simple in nature. The more complex a visual display becomes, the more difficult it is to understand. Simplicity is your friend as you try to show your audience an important idea, concept, or relationship.

Second, good visuals frequently explain relationships—that is, how one set of numbers or events relates to another. You can show how they're related at one moment in time (with a pie chart or bar graph, for example) or how they change over time (with a line graph).

Another characteristic of good visuals is that they use color effectively. Very few people tend to have exactly the same taste or preference for colors, but almost everyone will say that they appreciate when colors are used meaningfully and consistently. Using red numbers or bars to indicate a loss and black images to represent a profit has a readily understood meaning for most audiences. Using a simple *legend*, or explanation of color use on your charts and graphs, is one way to assure consistency and simplicity in your visual aids.

**Good visuals frequently explain relationships—that is, how one set of numbers or events relates to another.**

Finally, good presentation visuals are easy to set up, display, and transport. And, above all else, they consistently reinforce the spoken message. You can't afford to say one thing and show another. The visual and vocal messages must work together to reach your audience.

# TRUTH
42

## Understand visual images before you use them

A wide range of visual elements is available to help you illustrate and make your point in a presentation. Let's focus on five of them here. Choosing the right visual depends on your message and the comparisons you hope to make.

1. **The pie chart**—This is among the most common of graphic support ideas, perhaps because its design is so basic and easy to understand. A pie chart consists of a circle (or pie shape) with triangular components created by

> Choosing the right visual depends on your message and the comparisons you hope to make.

drawing lines from the center point to the edge of the circle. The purpose of a pie chart is to show the size of each part as a percentage of the whole. The source of revenues in an annual budget, for example, is easily represented in a pie chart. The general advice on constructing these charts is this: No more than half a dozen components, each colored or shaded differently, and the most important or largest component should begin at the twelve o'clock position and the rest should move in descending clockwise order.

2. **The bar chart**—This familiar graphic shows comparisons across a horizontal scale. The vertical axis of a bar chart labels the items being compared or measured, while the horizontal axis shows the frequency or measurement. Bar charts customarily show item comparisons and provide a viewer with relative size at a glance. The best advice is to keep the number of horizontal bars to six or fewer and to use color to identify key components.

3. **The column chart**—This is a more common variation of the bar chart, featuring vertical columns. The column chart shows changes over time, while the pie chart and bar chart each make comparisons at one moment in time. The horizontal scale, usually labeled across the bottom of the chart, shows progression in time with earlier dates to the left and later dates to the right. The vertical axis shows the measurement that's being compared. You can compare

two items with a column chart by pairing those items in differently colored (or shaded) columns and showing how each measured at a particular moment in time.

4.  **The line graph**—This frequently used graph helps to visualize a trend over time and shows whether that trend is increasing, decreasing, fluctuating, or remaining constant. These graphs are usually constructed with data points that are connected to one another across the chart from left to right. As with a column chart, the horizontal axis is used to display time from earlier (on the left) to later (on the right). The vertical axis reveals the measurement used, such as closing stock price or quarterly revenues.

5.  **The scatter diagram**—This graphic is closely related to a line graph, but depicts a different kind of data. Whereas a line graph might take one data point per time period (say, each day) and connect each entry with a solid line to show a trend over time, a scatter diagram shows all data at a single point in time. This diagram shows the correlation of one variable to another, or the relationship to a pattern you would expect to see. The horizontal and vertical axes are each used to scale a different variable, or item to be compared.

The important thing to remember is this: The message of your talk and the type of comparison you hope to make determines the type of chart that you select to illustrate your presentation.

TRUTH

43

Choose the right visual

Gene Zelazny, the director of visual communication for McKinsey & Company, says the best approach to choosing the right visual for your presentation is a simple, three-step process: first, determine your message; next, identify the comparison; and, finally, select the chart form.

"Choosing a chart form without a message in mind," he says, "is like trying to color-coordinate your wardrobe while blindfolded." Choosing the correct chart form depends on clearly knowing what message you want to deliver in your presentation. The data (dollars, percentages, gallons, and so on) doesn't determine the chart. Nor does the measure (return on investment, examination scores, and so on) determine which chart you should choose. Rather, it's *your* message, what *you* want to show, the specific point *you* want to make.

The second step is to identify the type of comparison you want to make. Graphic design experts have identified five basic kinds of visual comparisons:

## Identify the type of comparison you want to make.

1. **Component comparison**—In this form of comparison, you show the size of each part as a percentage of the total. For example, "Two-thirds of all mortgage loans were made within a five-county area." Or "Five sales representatives accounted for nearly 60 percent of all revenues during August."

2. **Item comparison**—In an item comparison, you hope to show how things rank: Are they about the same or is one more or less than the others? For example, "In January, the Northeast region exceeded the natural gas use of all other regions." Or "During the second quarter of this fiscal year, Morgan Stanley ranked third among all investment banks in IPO activity."

3. **Time-series comparison**—In this comparison, you don't care about which part of the total an item might be, nor are you concerned with how they're ranked. You focus on how they change over time and whether the trend is increasing, decreasing, fluctuating, or remaining constant. For example, "Airline seating capacity has declined sharply since

September, 2001." Or "Interest rates have risen slowly over the past two years."

**4.    Frequency-distribution comparison**—A comparison of this type shows how many items are distributed into a series of progressive numerical ranges. For example, "More than 30 percent of U.S. adults earn between $30,000 and $40,000 per year." Or "Nearly 60 percent of adults 55 and older read a daily newspaper."

**5.    Correlation comparison**—A correlation comparison shows both how and the degree to which two items are related. For example, "CEO compensation tends to vary according to the market capitalization of their employer." Or "A slight relationship exists between years of experience and sales performance during February."

Selecting the right chart form is relatively easy, once you determine the content of your message and identify the type of comparison you want to make. You should use a pie chart to best show a component comparison. Item comparisons frequently benefit from either a bar chart (horizontal) or a column chart (vertical). A time-series comparison typically employs either a column chart or a line graph, as could a frequency comparison. Finally, if you hope to make a correlation comparison, then use either a two-direction bar chart or a scatter diagram.

Selecting the right visual makes it easier for your audience to understand the sort of comparison you're hoping to draw and makes it more likely they'll understand and appreciate the message you're trying to convey.

# TRUTH

## 44

# Use PowerPoint effectively

In most organizations today, PowerPoint is the de facto program used for business presentations. It's also increasingly used for business reporting because business readers have little time for lengthy reports or memos. PowerPoint requires an author to be both succinct and to the point.

PowerPoint dominates business communication for other reasons, as well: it's relatively easy to use; you can store and transmit your data or speech electronically; and you can easily project it to groups of almost any size, yet print it in on any printer, so it serves as a basic record of a talk or presentation.

But the program's strengths are also its weaknesses. Many commentators and experts complain about the use of cryptic bulleted lists, text-heavy paragraphs, meaningless clip art, and data graphics that are all but impossible to decipher. Although PowerPoint is easy to use, using it well is a challenge.

To get the full benefit of the program, a communicator must apply principles of good visual communication. A PowerPoint presentation reaches its full potential only when it captures and focuses the audience's attention, communicates information at a glance, and uses visual techniques to help the audience follow and understand the message.

To design an effective PowerPoint show, you must do three things:

1. **Create an effective template**—The best way to create visual consistency in PowerPoint is to design or choose a template that includes key visual elements on a master slide. This template includes colors, fonts (and font sizes), bullets, headers, footers, and margins. This way, these visual elements remain

> A PowerPoint presentation reaches its full potential only when it captures and focuses the audience's attention, communicates information at a glance, and uses visual techniques to help the audience follow and understand the message.

consistent from slide to slide, without variation. Consider a simple look for your slides. Use basic, solid backgrounds that give your images a clear, crisp, and uncluttered appearance. Make sure the colors you select have sufficient contrast, avoid ornate bullets, and keep your font sizes consistent throughout. Position your headlines flush left and don't capitalize more than the first word or proper nouns in your heads and bullet points.

2.   **Design coherent and readable slides**—At its best, a PowerPoint slide should quickly capture and focus the audience's attention. It should not invite the audience to read in detail; an audience that's reading is not listening to the presenter. It also should not confuse the audience by presenting content that doesn't clearly support the headline or relate to other ideas on the slide. Consider writing a headline that tells a story, like a newspaper headline. Rather than saying, "Sales revenues by region," you might write, "Southwest region leads in sales revenue." Ideally, the headline of a slide raises an expectation, and the body of the slide fulfills that expectation by presenting material in the most effective form: bullet lists, tables, diagrams, photos, illustrations, or some combination of those. Beyond that, remember to leave plenty of white space and make the text easy to read. Viewers need empty space to help them focus their vision, so if your slide is too crowded, your audience may feel overwhelmed and see nothing at all. It's better to write a few concise points than to include whole paragraphs.

3.   **Signal the presentation's flow**—Finally, help your audience to understand the flow of your presentation by signaling them with one of several visual devices. Agenda or divider slides can cue the audience about large sections of your presentation. Road signs or small text elements—typically in the upper-right corner of each slide—can signal where you are in your talk. And, of course, your headlines can signal a logical flow as well.

PowerPoint is a great tool for illustrating and delivering your message, if you use it properly. Keep it simple, clean, and uncluttered. Don't overwhelm your audience with flying bullet points, transitions, and sound effects. Make sure everything you enter on a slide is there for one purpose: to support and explain your message to the audience.

# TRUTH

## 45

# Consider speaking without visuals

Can I speak without visuals? Yes, of course. That's the basic difference between a public speaker and a narrator. Some speaking situations call for visual aids, and you'll want to make certain that you illustrate the content of your speech appropriately. Other speaking occasions either don't require visual support or are better served without it. I can't imagine John F. Kennedy, Martin Luther King, Jr., or Winston Churchill using PowerPoint to illustrate a talk. They were, of course, political orators, not businessmen. But the point is the same: Don't overdo the visual aids.

Some executives have been known to ban PowerPoint entirely from their company presentations. That seems like an overreaction, but you can easily understand how those feelings came about. A colleague once showed me some discouraging written critiques of a presentation he gave to a supervisory development course: "Overhead avalanche," read one. "Death by PowerPoint," said another. My advice to him was simple: Use fewer slides; make sure they reinforce only key points; and make certain you do not overdo the basics, including color, transitions, type fonts, motion, and sound effects. These things are typically overwhelming or distracting for the audience.

Keep in mind that you may be the best visual of all. "Good leaders understand that *they* are the best visual," says Judith Humphrey, president of the Humphrey Group, a Toronto-based firm that specializes in executive speech training. "They instinctively know that their message will come through best if the audience looks at them and listens to them—with no distractions." Her recommendations

## You may be the best visual of all.

include stepping out from behind the podium and making yourself a focal point of the speech. "If you are committed and engaged, the audience can see it in your face, in your gestures, in the way you walk, in the way you stand, in the way you hold your head high."

"Here's the key," says Humphrey. "Great speaking is really about great thinking. People can be persuaded by the passion you have for your ideas, but only if they can see you." In a darkened room, she says, the audience is focused on the slides and not on you. "But, if you're willing to step forward, look them in the eyes, and show your conviction for those ideas, people will be more inclined to believe you." You could e-mail those slides to your audience, but when you speak to them in person, you become an important part of the speech itself. "If so much information is processed visually," she adds, "that's all the more reason to make yourself visual."

**In a darkened room, the audience is focused on the slides and not on you.**

This may mean inserting an occasional blank slide in your PowerPoint presentation to create an opportunity for you to explain the main point of your talk or show why it might be particularly important for your audience to act on what you just told them. It may mean stepping forward, out of the shadows, so that your audience can see you. And, of course, it means taking advantage of the opportunity to create a personal bond between you and at least a few selected members of the audience who can act as proxies for the rest. The more personal and human this bond, the greater the chance your audience will understand your commitment to the ideas in the speech and respond in the way you hope.

Speaking without visual support has risks, particularly if the information you're speaking about is detailed, complex, technical, or focused on trends. Spoken numbers, especially if they're precise, can quickly overwhelm an audience that has no other reference point. If you plan to speak without visuals, you may want to round off your numbers: "More than two-and-a-half million..." or "Less than four percent..." You also want to make sure you repeat your main points frequently and summarize in a way that helps the audience remember and understand what you're saying. If you rehearse carefully and know your subject well, speaking without visual support may help to bring you and your audience closer together.

# TRUTH

## 46

# Assess the mood of your audience

As you know by now, one of the key ways to prepare for a presentation is to learn all you can about your prospective audience. Two things you most want to know about your audience are what they know about the topic of your talk and how they feel about it.

Here are a few ideas for assessing their likely reaction to what you have to say:

**Research your audience in advance**—Knowing who they are and what they believe can help you win them over and keep you from making serious errors along the way. Colin Quinn, the comedian from *Saturday Night Live* recently spoke to a distinguished society of senior public relations and communications professionals at their annual spring meeting in New York. Without any prior research on the group he was speaking to, Quinn stood up after dinner and used his customary nightclub act on the crowd. Not only was the material inappropriate for the audience and occasion, but he also insulted the public relations profession several times. Several attendees asked afterward if the society could get its money back from the comedian.

Look online, talk to people in the group that you're going to address and find out what their values are, and look for ways to connect your message to the principles and ideals of the people in your audience.

**Talk to those who invited you to speak**—The people likely to be most helpful in your research are those who asked you to address this group. Find out the purpose of their meeting, why they selected you as a speaker, and what they expect from your talk. Ask about previous speakers and the topics of their presentations. Find out if the group had strong reactions—positive or negative—to other speakers and plan your remarks accordingly.

> Two things you most want to know about your audience are what they know about the topic of your talk and how they feel about it.

**Meet with people as they enter the room**—You should arrive early before giving a talk and get to know the presentation venue. That's also an opportunity for you to meet people as they enter the room, introduce yourself, and get to know something about them. Knowing a little bit more about their experience, interests, and expectations can help to humanize you and make you seem more personal to an important segment of the audience.

**Look for nonverbal signals**—As you speak, do your best to make and maintain contact with your audience. Look them in the eyes and reposition yourself as needed so that you address all members of the group, no matter where they are sitting or standing. Watch for signals that reveal their level of interest in your presentation: head nods, smiles, facial expressions, or furrowed brows. Body posture can tell you a lot: If they slump down in their chairs, fold their arms, or begin looking at their watches (or cell phones), that's not good. You want them to sit up, lean forward, tune in, and watch what you're doing.

If things aren't going well, then shift gears and change your approach. Part of the problem could be your delivery: You may need to speak up, increase the pitch in your voice, and avoid a monotone. Or you may want to approach the audience or gesture more. At some point, you may even need to shorten your talk and conclude your remarks, repeating what you think is most important for them to know and driving home your main point one last time. Cue the audience as you do this, telling them that this is "the one thing I think you most need to know about this subject...."

**Reassure them that you have something in common**—Most audiences are looking for a reason to like you, so give them one. Talk about what you share in common: Your values, beliefs, ideas, approach to life, or actions that you know they'll approve of. Even disagreeable audiences are polite long enough to hear what you have to say if you can show them that you're on their side on issues they think are important. Sincerely acknowledging their side of the argument is one effective way to do that.

# TRUTH

## 47

# Answer the audience's questions

Sometimes audience members are not permitted to ask questions. In that case, your task is to anticipate their concerns and deal with them in your prepared remarks. If the format of your presentation allows for questions following your talk, then you should prepare for that. Here's the truth about handling questions:

- **Listen to the question**—Patiently listen to the entire question and focus on both the content of the question and the reason it's being asked. Don't interrupt the questioner, even if you're pretty sure you know where the question is heading. Listen to all of it thoughtfully and then reply.

- **Pause to think about your answer**—If you reply to a question with a canned response, the audience will know it. Don't act so eager to reply that your answer sounds scripted. Try your best to create the impression that you are responding to *this* question from *this* audience member and, if possible, personalize your reply.

- **Don't repeat the question**—If the questioner doesn't have access to a microphone and others in the audience cannot hear the question, go ahead and repeat it. Otherwise, just think about the question and formulate a reply that addresses the issue that was raised.

- **Don't drift off topic**—Answer only the question that's asked and make your reply as specific as possible. On the other hand, the conventional advice to politicians and public spokesmen is, "If someone asks you a question that you cannot answer, then answer a question you wish they had asked." The floor is still yours and you should focus on issues that are important to you and your reasons for being there, but remember that the questioner still deserves a straightforward, honest response to the question.

> The questioner deserves a straightforward, honest response to the question.

- **Address the whole audience**—The question-and-answer period is not the time to begin a personal conversation with one individual in the audience. Try to address your reply to the whole audience, not just to the questioner. That way, they'll all still feel included.

■ **Answer questions completely**—Stay with the question until you answer it fully. That means putting yourself in the shoes of the audience member who was brave enough to get up and ask you a question. Try to understand what motivates the question and how she feels about the subject. Give as complete an answer as you think you can.

■ **Don't make the questioner feel dumb**—There is no such thing as a dumb question. If someone honestly wants to know more about the subject of your speech, take the time and make the effort to address his concerns. Many people don't know as much about this subject as you do, and they might not feel the same way about it. Make the audience member feel smart for asking you something important.

> There really is no such thing as a dumb question.

■ **Don't dismiss a question as irrelevant**—Some questions may seem off topic or less relevant than others to your reasons for speaking, but go ahead and respond anyway. Treat the question and questioner seriously and your audience will appreciate it.

■ **Don't dismiss a questioner as unimportant**—The question-and-answer period is the moment for a junior or less prestigious member of the audience to stand and ask about your speech. Treat each member of the audience with respect and dignity, and you'll win the respect of others in the room.

■ **Don't let one person dominate the questioning**—If someone has a flood of questions for you, answer patiently and briefly, then break eye contact and make contact with someone else. Ask for other questions.

■ **What if you don't have an answer?**—Say so. Give the person credit for raising an issue you didn't think about and offer to find an answer. Don't make something up on the spot; offer to get the answer and get back to them; then keep your promise.

# TRUTH

48

# Handle hostility with confidence

Audience hostility generally comes in two forms. First, hostile activities or actions from them might include distractions, annoyances, and rude or inconsiderate behavior. And second, audience members may ask questions that challenge your authority, question your competence, or are openly hostile to your subject or point of view. Let's deal with distractions first.

**Late arrivals**—Keep your promise to start on time unless a key decision-maker is not yet in the room and starting without him is pointless. If you start on time, you may find that some audience members arrive late and create a disturbance as they find a seat and get settled. The best plan is generally to ignore all of that. They'll settle down in a few moments and you can move on. If the late arrival is an important person who deserves an update, you may wish to offer a brief recap of key points already discussed and then move on to your next point. Keep in mind that the majority of late arrivals are as embarrassed or self-conscious about the moment as you are.

**Side conversations**—Some audience-to-audience conversations are useful, like when people help others in the room catch up or show them where to find certain information in your handouts. Other conversations, though, are an indication that the audience is growing restless. If just two people in a conversation are a problem, you might try strolling closer to them without looking directly at them. As the audience begins to look in your direction as you move, the talkers will grow conscious that others are watching them, too, and likely will end the conversation.

If the audience is sending nonverbal signals that they're restless, unhappy, or that their energy is flagging, you may need to provide them with a break for a few minutes. If that's not part of the presentation plan, you can acknowledge that there are other points of view or that some may disagree with your perspective.

> If just two people in a conversation are a problem, you might try strolling closer to them without looking directly at them.

Then, tackle the disagreement head-on and explain why you chose a particular viewpoint.

**Hostile or accusatory questions**—If you receive questions from an audience member that are openly hostile to you or your material, address the issue that is raised and not the tone of the question. An angry or hostile response from you plays into the hands of those who hope to discredit you or challenge your competence. Behave politely and professionally, but persist in explaining your perspective.

Sometimes audience members have an ulterior motive or an agenda they hope to advance. Acknowledge the viewpoint, explain why you disagree with it, and move on. Keep your answers to one breath or one brief point. Don't offer audience members an opportunity to debate you or give a speech of their own. If a questioner won't give up and keeps asking you hostile questions, say "I think I've responded in a way that answers your question as best I can. Are there other questions or observations from the audience?" Then, turn and make eye contact with someone else, perhaps someone with a raised hand or expectant facial expression.

> Don't offer audience members an opportunity to debate you or give a speech of their own.

Actor-director Mel Gibson found himself at the center of controversy while he was addressing film students at California State University. A professor specializing in Mayan literature accused Gibson of stereotyping the subjects of his film, *Apocalypto*. The questioner obviously had a viewpoint that differed dramatically from Gibson's and her intentions were both hostile and accusatory. The director could have deflected criticism by acknowledging her view, or their different viewpoints at the very least, and then moving on to another question. Instead, he chose to argue the point with her, raising his voice and using language many considered inappropriate. Don't let a heckler get the best of you; seek common ground in your reply whenever possible.

# Turn a tough question to your advantage by connecting it to key points or central themes in your own talk.

Finally, turn a tough question to your advantage by connecting it to key points or central themes in your own talk. Return to the principal issues of your talk and reinforce these themes by linking them to the needs and interests of the audience. Remember, if you stay calm, patient, and good-humored, the audience will give you the benefit of the doubt and appreciate your professionalism.

# TRUTH

## 49

# Know as much as possible
# about the location

Long before the day of your talk, check on all of the most important details about the location and plan to arrive just a little early. This extra time gives you an opportunity to look at and think about a number of issues regarding the location and setup of your presentation room.

**Date, time, and location**—Where are you supposed to be? When is your talk scheduled to begin? If you are unfamiliar with the location, find out as much as you can about it in advance. Figure out the best route to your speaking location. Find out where to park and where the room or auditorium for your presentation is located.

> Plan to arrive just a little early.

**Room layout**—Walking into the room with no idea of how it will be organized is unwise. Don't depend on others to set up the room to your satisfaction either. If possible, arrive early and arrange the room the way you like it. It's your speech, so take charge of the room.

**Microphone and acoustics**—Try out the sound system in advance. If you have to wear a wireless mike, find out exactly what you need to do to make it work. Decide beforehand whether you are willing to speak without a sound system if it fails or wait for someone to repair it.

**Visual aids**—Check out the screen, the placement of your projector, and the system you plan to use to support your talk. Make sure the image is focused, centered, and visible to the people in the back row.

**Stage**—Take a moment to find out how to get on and off the stage; where the sound projection limits are in the room; and location of the trap doors, cables, and high-risk footing. Figure out where the stage is and how close your podium is positioned to the edge. More than one professional speaker or performer has literally fallen off the edge of a stage or raised platform because he didn't pay attention to the boundaries. A raised platform with a curtain behind you is particularly dangerous and deserves your close attention before you begin the presentation.

**Time limit**—Double-check with your host on the time limit for your talk and then abide by it. Don't disappoint by ending your talk early or by speaking beyond your allotted time.

**Lectern**—Find out where the podium is situated and, if possible, whether you can move beyond it and walk around the front of the room. Check to see if the lectern has a light, make sure it works, and determine whether it is bright enough for you to see your notes.

**Notes**—Don't trust anyone else with your speech. If you work from a script or detailed notes, personally hang onto them. Review them beforehand, but don't make a point of pouring over them just as your host is about to introduce you. Bring a backup copy of your speech and keep it handy in your coat pocket or briefcase, just in case something happens to your first copy.

> Bring a backup copy of your speech.

**Lights**—Determine whether the overhead lighting will wash out a projected image on the screen. Are the lights bright enough for people to see you and whatever handouts you provide? Are they dim enough to allow the audience to see your visual aids?

**Try it out**—Use the microphone, check out the projector, walk across the stage, and examine the effect of your visual aids from the back of the room. Determine whether you are visible and audible from all parts of the room. Gain some confidence by knowing where you'll stand and what it feels like before you actually begin.

TRUTH

50

# Use the microphone to your advantage

Unless you're speaking in a small room to just a few people, you may want to consider what a public address system might do for your presentation. If you have to strain your voice to speak loudly enough so everyone can hear you, then you need a PA system. If you can speak comfortably in conversational tones and are clearly understood by all in the room, then you probably don't need amplification.

Using a microphone can seem intimidating at first, but once you try it out and grow accustomed to the amplified sound of your voice, you'll be fine. Here are a few ideas to keep in mind as you approach the microphone for the first time:

**Understand the microphone type you're using**—Microphones come in two basic types: wired and wireless. *A wireless mike* permits you to move around freely, unrestrained by cables and cords. The disadvantage is that wireless mikes are more sensitive to interference and are dependent on batteries (which may not be fresh). A *wired mike* is highly dependable and produces good sound quality, but you must know where the cable is at all times so that you don't trip over it.

**Understand how to use a wireless microphone**—Wireless mikes come in two types: clip-on and hand-held. *Clip-on mikes* are small, lightweight, and easy to use. For men, the best place to fasten a clip-on mike is to your necktie or shirt, as high as possible, about three or four inches below your chin. For women, the advice is the same, but note that clip-on mikes are sensitive and will pick up any noises from contact with necklaces, jewelry, and name badges. Clipping the mike to your jacket lapel will work, but you may experience some voice fade as you turn your head away from the side on which you're wearing the mike. Once it's in place, just switch it on when you're ready to begin your talk and don't touch it. Clip-on mikes typically come with a wire that connects them to a small transmitter and battery pack. You can put that in your pocket or fasten it to your belt if you like. Do whatever makes you most comfortable or creates the least distraction. *Hand-held wireless mikes* typically have an on-off switch on the bottom that you need to activate when you're

> Clip-on mikes are sensitive and will pick up any noises from contact with necklaces, jewelry, and name badges.

ready to begin your presentation. Hold the mike about six inches from your mouth when speaking. Don't hold it directly in front of your face, because that's not necessary for you to be heard and because this creates a visual distraction for the audience. If you need to clear your throat, hold the mike down at your side. If you need to speak to someone without the audience hearing any of what you say, switch the mike off and wait for the small light to go off (or change from green to red).

**Understand how to use a wired microphone**—Wired microphones come in two general styles: mobile and fixed. A *mobile mike* is attached to a stand that permits you to hold something else in your hands, but if you use the stand, you can't move more than a foot or so away from the tip of the mike without experiencing some fade. If you want to move about with a mobile, wired mike, coil up the cable so that it can unwind as you move freely about the stage. The cord is a mess by the time you're done speaking, but it is certainly easier to begin with the cable in one place. If you're using a *fixed microphone*, which is attached to a podium or lectern, you have to remain close by and speak into the mike without getting too close (so your voice doesn't sound loud and distorted) or too far away (no one will be able to hear you). As you move your arms to gesture, make sure that you look both left and right to make eye contact with as many people in the audience as possible while staying close to the podium.

**Try it out**—Try out a microphone when you first arrive, if that's possible. A brief practice run with the mike at normal volume eliminates surprises and distractions from your message later on. As you speak for the first time, offer a greeting to the audience, explain why you're happy to be there with them, and speak in your normal tone and volume. An audio technician (or your host) is usually available to help if you have problems, too.

> Try out a microphone when you first arrive.

**Be careful of feedback**—When a microphone is placed in front of amplified speakers, the sound from those speakers will feed back into the mike, creating that incredibly annoying high-pitched squeal that brings everything to a halt. If you move around with a microphone (wired or wireless), make sure you know how far you can go into the audience or forward on the stage without creating that squeal. Look for markings or positions on the stage to guide you as you rehearse your first few lines with a live mike.

Once the microphone is working and you're comfortable with how you sound, don't worry about your voice. Speak in your natural, normal tone and try your best to engage the audience.

# TRUTH

## 51

## Know your limits

Some things that you should know well before you enter a presentation venue are your audience, your subject, and your reasons for speaking. In addition, you should also know your limits. In particular, before you get up to speak, you should think about limitations of time, space, and your own expertise.

**Understand your time limits—** There are several good reasons to know in advance how long you'll speak. First, of course, you may not be the only speaker on the program. You may, in fact, be one of several people scheduled to speak to this audience on this occasion, and you

> You should think about limitations of time, space, and your own expertise.

simply cannot risk taking other people's allocated speaking time. If you're given 20 minutes, plan to use 19. If questions-and-answers are an important part of your program, plan to speak for two-thirds of the time allocated for your talk and then devote one-third of the time to audience questions.

Time limits are important for other reasons, too. Your hosts may arrange for an audiovisual crew to record your remarks. They work on a schedule and are prepared to record your talk for the allocated time. Don't throw them a curveball and speak longer than your scheduled time. Finally, your audience has a set of expectations about how long this will take, and they'll want you to deliver on your promise. Don't test their patience by keeping them in the lecture hall or auditorium long past the scheduled timeframe of your presentation.

**Understand your space limits—**You should know well in advance of your introduction just how far you can maneuver on the stage or dais, being careful not to step too close to the forward edge (or back) of the speaking platform. A few years ago, I watched a speaker work toward the back of a small platform at a luncheon in Denver. She was fine until she took *one more* step back and fell off the dais. Unfortunately for her, the microphone was still live and it captured the pain and frustration of the moment. The rest of the speech didn't go well.

The second principal reason for knowing how far you can move around the stage or how far out into the audience you can safely walk is to prevent audio feedback—that annoying squeal that has the audience wincing and the speaker wondering what's gone wrong. Ask your host or the audio-visual technician about space limits before you're introduced and plan accordingly.

**Understand the limits of your expertise**—In the heat of the moment, particularly in response to a pointed or specific question, you're sometimes tempted to offer opinions about subjects you don't really know that well. Recognizing the limits of your subject-matter expertise and then working within those limits are vitally important. Jody Powell, the press secretary during Jimmy Carter's presidency, was once asked if he'd learned anything in the course of his job that he didn't know when he was first appointed. "Oh, yeah," he replied. "I learned that, almost invariably, there was someone in the room who knew more about the subject than I did." Powell related the story of a White House luncheon at which he was asked to speak, without realizing that the people in the room were all experts on the subject he was asked to talk about. "That's a tough lesson," he said, "but humility and a willingness to say 'I don't know the answer to that' will keep you from genuine embarrassment."

Knowing your own limits, including time, space, and subject matter expertise limitations can keep you from saying things you'll later regret or have to apologize for. Working within your own comfort zone keeps you confident, sincere, and professional, which is, of course, exactly what your audience expects of you.

# References

### Truth 6

Bloom, Benjamin S., Taxonomy of Educational Objectives.

### Truth 7

Personal interview with Joan Finnessy, conducted at the University of Notre Dame.

### Truth 9

Gordon Bethune speech, provided by Continental Airlines.

### Truth 11

Munter, Mary. *Guide to Managerial Communication*, Sixth Edition. Upper Saddle River, NJ: Prentice Hall, 2002, pp. 10-17.

### Truth 14

Hamlin, Sonya. *How to Talk So People Listen: Connecting In Today's Workplace*. New York, NY: Collins, 2006.

### Truth 16

Nichols, R.G. "Listening Is a 10-Part Skill," in Huseman, R.C., et al, eds., *Readings in Interpersonal and Organizational Communication*. Boston: Holbrook Press, 1969, pp. 472-479.

Crossen, C. "The Crucial Question for These Noisy Times May Just Be: 'Huh?'" *Wall Street Journal*, July 10, 1997, p. A1. Reprinted by permission of *The Wall Street Journal*. Copyright 1997, Dow Jones & Company, Inc. All rights reserved worldwide.

Goleman, D. *Emotional Intelligence*. New York: Bantam Books, 1995, p. 145.

### Truth 20

Mulcahy, Anne, in an address to students, faculty, and alumni, Mendoza College of Business, University of Notre Dame, Saturday, September 6, 2003.

### Truth 22

Lucas, Stephen E. *The Art of Public Speaking*, 9th edition.  New York, NY: McGraw-Hill, Inc. (2006).

## Truth 24

Personal interview with Stephen Hayes, a business-services librarian at the University of Notre Dame, June 22, 2007.

## Truth 26

Winerman, Lea. "Thin Slices of Life," *APA Monitor*. www.apa.org/monitor/mar05/slices.html

## Truth 40

Knapp, M. and J. Hall, *Nonverbal Communication in Human Interaction*, Third Edition. Fort Worth, TX: Holt Rinehart and Winston, 1992, p. 27.

## Truth 43

Zelazny, Gene, in a classroom lecture to students and faculty, Mendoza College of Business, University of Notre Dame, Monday, October 9, 2006. (Zelazny, Gene. *Say It With Presentations*, 2nd edition. New York, NY: McGraw-Hill, Inc., 2006.)

## Truth 45

O'Rourke, James, *Management Communication*, Third Edition. Upper Saddle River, NJ: Prentice Hall, 2006, pp.116-117).

# Acknowledgments

A book such as this simply isn't possible without the help of many hands and minds. I'm deeply grateful to my publisher, Jennifer Simon of Pearson, for her diligent work and thoughtful approach to this series. I'm grateful, as well, to Russ Hall, Lori Lyons, and Carol Pogoni, who helped to transform rough copy into a polished manuscript.

I'm fortunate beyond measure to have colleagues in the Fanning Center at Notre Dame who provide me with good ideas, inspiration, confidence, and encouragement. Sandra Collins, Sondra Byrnes, and Cynthia Maciejczyk are simply the best. To my friends and colleagues in the Management Communication Association and the Arthur W. Page Society, I say thanks as well. Your unrestricted collegiality and extraordinary professional judgment make many things possible. I'm deeply grateful you're my friends.

And, finally, this wouldn't have been possible without the love, support, and conviction of my wife Pam, and my daughters Colleen, Molly, and Kathleen. Thanks. You're the reason I do things like this.

# About the Author

**James S. O'Rourke, IV** teaches management and corporate communication at the University of Notre Dame, where he is a Concurrent Professor of Management and the Arthur F. and Mary J. O'Neil Director of the Eugene D. Fanning Center for Business Communication. In a career spanning four decades, he has earned an international reputation in business and corporate communication. *Business Week* magazine has named him one of the "outstanding faculty" in Notre Dame's Mendoza College of Business.

In 2004, he was named as recipient of the Fifth Annual John A. Kaneb Teaching Award in the Mendoza College of Business and was recognized during the University's 159th Commencement exercises.

His publications include *Management Communication: A Case Analysis Approach* (Third edition, Prentice-Hall, 2007) and *Business Communication: A Framework for Success* (Thomson Learning, 2001). Professor O'Rourke is the senior editor of an eight-book series on Managerial Communication from Thomson Learning and is the principal author or directing editor of more than 130 management and corporate communication case studies.

Professor O'Rourke is a graduate of Notre Dame with advanced degrees from Temple University, the University of New Mexico, and a doctorate in Communication from the S. I. Newhouse School of Syracuse University. He has held faculty appointments in such schools as the United States Air Force Academy, the Defense Information School, the United States Air War College, and the Communications Institute of Ireland. He was a Gannett Foundation Teaching Fellow at Indiana University in the 1980s and a graduate student in language and history at Christ's College, Cambridge University in England during the 1970s. He has delivered invited lectures at leading universities in Denmark, Switzerland, the United Kingdom, Germany, Italy, and Singapore.

Professor O'Rourke is a trustee of both The Arthur W. Page Society and the Institute for Public Relations. He is a member of the Reputation Institute and the Management Communication Association. He is also a regular consultant to *Fortune 500* and mid-size businesses throughout North America. Dr. O'Rourke and his wife, Pam, have three daughters: Colleen (St. Mary's College, 1994), Molly (Notre Dame, 2000), and Kathleen (Notre Dame, 2007).